TOTAL QUALITY

MANAGEMENT

IN

GOVERNMENT

STEVEN COHEN

RONALD BRAND

TOTAL QUALITY MANAGEMENT IN GOVERNMENT

A PRACTICAL GUIDE
FOR
THE REAL WORLD

Jossey-Bass Publishers • San Francisco

Substantial discounts on bulk quantities of Jossey-Bass books are available to corporations, professional associations, and other organizations. For details and discount information, contact the special sales department at Jossey-Bass Inc., Publishers. (415) 433-1740; Fax (415)433-0499.

For sales outside of the United States, contact Maxwell Macmillan International Publishing Group, 866 Third Avenue, New York, New York 10022.

Manufactured in the United States of America

The paper used in this book is acid-free and meets the State of California requirements for recycled paper (50 percent recycled waste, including 10 percent postconsumer waste), which are the strictest guidelines for recycled paper currently in use in the United States.

Library of Congress Cataloging-in-Publication Data

Cohen, Steven, date.
    Total quality management in government : a practical guide for the real world / Steven Cohen, Ronald Brand. — 1st ed.
        p.   cm. — (The Jossey-Bass public administration series)
    Includes bibliographical references and index.
    ISBN 1-55542-539-9 (alk. paper)
    1. Public administration.   2. Total quality management.
  I. Brand, Ronald, date.   II. Title. III. Series.
JF1411.C64 1993
350.007'8—dc20

92-42281
CIP

FIRST EDITION
HB Printing 10 9 8 7 6 5 4 3 2

Code 9341

THE

JOSSEY-BASS

PUBLIC ADMINISTRATION

SERIES

To

Donna and Margaret

CONTENTS

PREFACE

Concepts of quality management are creating a quiet revolution in American industry and increasingly in American government. Industry is in a life-and-death struggle in a new global economy, while government is under constant pressure to deliver more services with fewer resources. Workers are encouraged to analyze and improve their own work processes in organizations as diverse as International Paper and the New York City Department of Parks and Recreation. The results are dramatic: increased quality and reduced costs. We are discovering that by "working smarter" we can regain our competitive advantage in the global marketplace.

Background

Japanese companies in a number of industries have surpassed American industry, by continuously improving the quality of goods and services and by meticulously and constantly improving workplace productivity. Traditionally, we have viewed productivity as a function of labor cost, capital and resource utilization, and technology. Advocates of total quality management (TQM) believe that at its base, improved quality increases productivity and reduces waste in producing, marketing, and supplying products or services.

Total quality management is a simple but revolutionary way of performing work. We define it as follows:

- *Total* implies applying the search for quality to every aspect of work, from identifying customer needs to aggressively evaluating whether the customer is satisfied.

- *Quality* means meeting and exceeding customer expectations.
- *Management* means developing and maintaining the organizational capacity to constantly improve quality.

Others may define TQM differently, but throughout this book, when we refer to TQM, this definition is the one we will follow.

W. Edwards Deming is one of the best-known gurus of total quality management. He believes that a passion for quality must be the cornerstone of a new American management philosophy. According to Deming, "Continual reduction in mistakes, continual improvement of quality, mean lower and lower costs" (Walton, 1986, p. 26). However, total quality management should not be confused with the traditional concept of quality control. The goal is not inspecting products or services in order to eliminate unsatisfactory ones. Instead, quality is built into the production process so that you do not have rejects. Waste that must be eliminated is caused by production mistakes. If you can reduce production mistakes, you thereby eliminate waste and reduce costs.

The lessons of quality management are slowly being introduced in government. The Federal Quality Institute was established in 1988 as a force to infuse government with quality principles. Cities such as Madison, Wisconsin, have incorporated total quality management into their daily work processes. In the federal Environmental Protection Agency (EPA), staff are trained in the techniques of quality management, a trend begun by Ronald Brand when he directed the EPA's Office of Underground Storage Tanks (OUST). Steven Cohen served as a management consultant to Brand during the years in which Brand ran OUST. *Total Quality Management in Government* conveys the lessons they learned in OUST's effort to implement total quality management in a federal regulatory program. Although a number of books discuss quality management in the private sector, little has been written about applying these concepts in a government setting. Government does not need to compete against foreign firms to survive, but it does face enormous challenges due to increasing demands and decreasing resources. TQM is one way to deal with those challenges.

One other definitional issue is important to note. Throughout this book, we use the terms *manager* and *employee* (or *worker*). However, in some situations managers are workers. Management is a form of work, and all managers work for someone and are employees (as opposed to managers) in that relationship. Therefore, even if you are a manager, the parts of the book that discuss workers' roles are important not only for your role of managing others but also for your role as someone else's employee.

Overview of the Contents

Chapter One provides the rationale for using TQM, discussing the steps necessary to make TQM operational in a public organization. The chapter then discusses why TQM has been used in Japan and in the private sector in the United States. Chapter One includes a discussion of why government and public managers should adopt TQM and concludes with a brief summary of the TQM movement in government.

Chapter Two introduces the core concepts of total quality management: (1) working with suppliers to ensure that the supplies utilized in work processes are designed for your use; (2) encouraging continual employee analysis of work processes to improve functioning and reduce process variation; and (3) establishing close communication with customers to identify and understand what they want and how they define quality. After defining terms, we then discuss why TQM is important and necessary to the individual manager.

Chapter Three discusses TQM as a form of major organizational change and innovation. Although TQM concepts appear to make sense, implementing them in a real-life organizational setting is difficult. This chapter discusses why organizational routines are so persistent and why bringing TQM into an organization is challenging. The implementation of TQM is the major theme of the book, and public managers should not underestimate the amount of effort involved. Chapter Three seeks to illuminate the concepts of TQM by contrasting them with traditional management concepts. Differences include the use of goals and management indicators—replacing concentration on arbitrary numerical indicators with a drive for improvement; the importance of work analysis; the methodology of work analysis (statistical process control and the search for variation); the use of employees as work and management analysts; the role of the manager as facilitator; and the use of teams and group work. The chapter begins by describing the new role that management plays within a TQM organization; management encourages and facilitates improvement. It discusses why management should use improvement goals rather than numerical quotas. This section addresses the need to reform management by objectives (MBO) to ensure that an organization's targets are based on the reality of current levels of performance. The chapter discusses the importance of workers' analysis of their own work and concludes by introducing a new paradigm for defining excellence in public management.

Chapter Three discusses the revolutionary aspects of TQM, while Chapter Four tells us why organizations tend to resist such revolutions. The chapter begins with an analysis of the relationship of stability to the bureaucratic form of organization. It then discusses how an organization's external environment and internal culture can both inhibit and engender change. The chapter is designed to provide public managers and students of public management with a sound understanding of why organizations resist change and why it is so difficult to implement major organizational change.

Chapter Five addresses "how to do it." The core of the TQM approach is the conviction that management must rely on the people who do the work to analyze and come up with improved methods of performing tasks. Quality is improved by dissecting, step by step, how work is performed. The workers must be given the authority and incentives to answer the following questions:

- Who is the customer for our work?
- Who does what when?

- Where do the supplies come from, and how can they be improved?
- What value is added to the product or service as it is passed from one worker to the next?
- What equipment is used to complete a task?
- How well does the equipment work? How often is it unavailable to do the work?
- How often are mistakes made that require redoing the work, that is, reconstructing the same product or service? What are the causes of these errors?
- How can you improve the process of performing tasks and thereby reduce redoing work? What specific modifications in the work process should be attempted?

W. Edwards Deming and others have advocated teaching workers to use a number of simple analytical and statistical tools to assess work. We agree that the tools are important. In *Total Quality Management in Government,* however, we have focused only on the most essential tools because we believe that in the early stage of analyzing work, sophisticated analytical tools are not necessary. Even worse, an emphasis on complex analytical techniques can discourage people and make it hard to get started. In Chapter Five, we introduce and define some basic tools, illustrate how they can be used to answer the questions listed above, and employ examples to illustrate their operation. These tools include

- Fishbone diagrams: a group method of determining the causes and effects of problems
- Pareto charts: a method of illustrating the relative importance of specific problems or variables, to help workers decide which of many problems to work on
- Flow charts: a method of describing the steps involved in performing tasks and producing products, which shows that all work is part of a process
- Run charts: a method of tracking progress over time
- Control charts: a method for determining how your system is operating

Now that you know what TQM is and why it is important, it is essential to understand the central role of managers in implementing TQM. Chapter Six details the part that public managers can play in introducing TQM in their own organizations. Most of the books that discuss quality management also discuss the importance of gaining commitment from the organization's top managers. Such commitment is difficult to come by in industry and is nearly impossible to obtain from politicians. Too often, this is used as an excuse for inaction on TQM, when there is room for improvement within your own organization.

Fortunately, it is possible to implement TQM in any part of an organization, as long as that part has its own set of tasks and some capacity for independent action. The manager's role is key. First, managers must study TQM, learning the core concepts and steps to change their style of managing workers. In particular, they need to allow employees to think through and implement improvements in work processes. Second, they must convince their employees to learn about and implement TQM. Next, managers must defend the use of TQM to outsiders in order to ensure that the results of employee-conducted work analysis will be used. This will sometimes require the courage to reject conventional wisdom and accepted practices. Finally, managers must establish an organizational culture that nurtures and reinforces continuous quality improvement.

Chapter Seven presents a case study that summarizes Ronald Brand's experiences in bringing TQM to his office at the EPA. The chapter describes how Brand came to learn about and utilize TQM and how he incorporated its lessons in his own office and in counterpart organizations at the regional, state, and local levels. We provide direction on how to train employees and develop the organizational routines needed to implement quality management.

A variety of TQM success stories from government settings are provided in Chapter Eight. It demonstrates that TQM can be and has been used in diverse settings. We also present cases ranging from those that require large-scale organizational effort to those that can be implemented by a few people on a modest scale.

The final chapter of the book, Chapter Nine, identifies the keys to success with TQM. Quality management is not a one-time, one-year program; once this new way of working is introduced in an organization, it must be constantly reinforced. First, there will always be people in the organization who are more comfortable with the old ways of working, and they may oppose TQM for some time. Second, it is likely that those outside the organization will not understand and may not support the new management system. You will probably have to persuade upper management to go along with the program, even though there are short-term risks. You must constantly support those employees who are willing to incorporate work analysis and TQM into their daily routine. Chapter Nine provides examples of efforts and unique strategies for such reinforcement. This chapter ties the book together by highlighting the major elements of a successful transformation from ordinary management to total quality management.

Purpose of the Book

Although one of the authors is a professor, the book does not intend to make a scholarly inquiry into the phenomenon of total quality management but rather to communicate the practical lessons we have learned about how to implement TQM in a government setting. While our focus is on government, these lessons are fully applicable to the private and nonprofit sectors. It is both a TQM primer and a "how-to-do-it" book. We are skeptical about formulaic conceptions of TQM and believe each organization must adapt TQM to its own environment. We have encountered consultants who think that TQM is a rigid set of procedures that organizations must adhere to scrupulously, and we think these consultants are wrong. We believe that, overall, TQM presents important concepts that are of great use to effective public managers, and we are eager to communicate these ideas to students and practitioners of public management. We have found that TQM works: it has helped organizations as disparate as the EPA's underground tank office and a dean's office at Columbia University.

TQM is not a cure-all, and it can be difficult to implement. In our view, however, it synthesizes some of the important lessons scholars and practitioners have learned about management in the past half-century and creates a useful, consistent management paradigm. TQM combines important lessons from the "hard" management science field of statistical process control with lessons from the "softer" management field that focuses on effective deployment and motivation of workers.

We have both had long careers in government at the city, state, and federal levels. We have tremendous respect for the people who make up the government workforce. Our fear is that many government organizations have been losing the respect of the citizenry because of the gap between current levels of performance and what is possible—even within the same resource levels.

Last year at a conference on pollution prevention, we heard a company describe an improved process they wanted to implement that would lessen pollution and save them money. However, they were struggling with a permit process that would take three years before they would be allowed to make the change. The state agency involved was present and admitted that the period of time for review and approval was three years.

Meanwhile, a computer technology firm in the same state books an order, builds the product, and ships it in the same day. This means that customers do not have to carry inventory, which saves money, reduces costs, and saves jobs. Our concern is that too many government organizations are or will become barriers to progress and to economic revitalization. We also see consumers obtaining new and more responsive services in many areas of their lives. This is creating the expectation that they should be just as well served in the public sector. Some government organizations are meeting this challenge, and more need to do so. TQM can help significantly.

Total Quality Management in Government is concerned with providing practical insight in order to solve real-world problems. It focuses on the sometimes mundane, but often critical, details of how work is accomplished and how organizations change their routines and methods of working.

Acknowledgments

Many people helped us as we learned about total quality management and explored how to bring it into a public organization. Ronald Brand acknowledges William Conway, James Copley, and Ellen Kendall of Conway Quality for providing his introduction to TQM. Their counsel highlighted the importance of focusing on value-added work and elimination of waste.

Both of us acknowledge the extraordinary efforts of everyone in the Office of Underground Storage Tanks at the U.S. Environmental Protection Agency. Everyone in the OUST program helped by encouraging us, viewing the work objectively, and finding wonderful new ways to improve it. A few people became eager TQM practitioners and advocates and helped sustain the effort to bring this way of working to the EPA's programs and customers. To those advocates, including Barbara Elkus, David Hamnett, Steven McNeely, David O'Brien, Connie Riley, Thomas Schruben, and Louise Wise, we offer special thanks.

Ronald Brand also thanks F. James McCormick of the EPA and Robert Cahill, formerly of the EPA and now at the Federal Quality Institute. These two "debating partners" helped him to develop and refine many of the ideas that brought TQM to OUST. Brand also thanks Roy Sutton and the people of W. B. Goode Company, Richmond, Virginia, for continuing to teach him practical lessons.

Our gratitude goes also to Helga Butler, who insisted on serving customers and communicating with them clearly. Some of the ideas in the book reflect her views of the realities of implementing TQM. Her continuing efforts to genuinely practice TQM have reinforced our conviction about its applicability to all types of government work. Thanks also go to Alvin Morris of the EPA Philadelphia Regional Office, who served as a support and inspiration through his efforts in TQM.

We also acknowledge the OUST regional program managers who learned and struggled with TQM and tried to apply it in the field. Especially heartening were the improvements achieved by the participants in the state underground tank programs who through their efforts taught us how many barriers had to be, and could be, overcome. Of the team of consultants we worked with, we would especially like to thank Gardner Shaw and Thomas Ingersoll.

Public managers around the country inspired us as we wrote *Total Quality Management in Government.* We acknowledge Commissioner Betsy Gottbaum, Assistant Commissioner Edward Norris, Deputy Commissioner William Dalton, and Parks Quality Coordinator Warren DeLuca at New York City's Department of Parks and Recreation. At Columbia University's Graduate Program in Public Policy and Administration, the help of Professors William Eimicke and Jacob Ukeles was appreciated as well as the work of Dorothy Chambers, Nancy Degnan, and Lorraine Wolfenson. A special note of thanks goes to Andrea Boone, our research assistant during the always challenging closing phases of this project. Steven Cohen is also grateful to John Ruggie, dean of Columbia University's School of International and Public Affairs, for encouraging him to combine the roles of university administrator, government consultant, researcher, writer, and professor.

We also acknowledge the support and forbearance of our families as we worked on this book. Ronald Brand thanks his wife, Margaret, his indispensable partner, for her constant support, understanding, and encouragement. Her many years of management experience in the health care field made her contributions especially significant, and her questions clarified much of the thinking that went into this book.

Steven Cohen thanks his wife, Donna Fishman, for her love and support. Through three book projects, she has always been there with understanding and help. Cohen also thanks his daughter Gabriella Rose Cohen, his parents, Marvin and Shirley, his brother Robert, and his sisters Judith and Myra.

We think this book can help make government work better, and therefore we acknowledge the millions of dedicated public servants who are trying their best, every day, to deliver excellent service.

February 1993

Steven Cohen
New York, New York

Ronald Brand
Richmond, Virginia

THE AUTHORS

S*teven Cohen* is associate dean of the School of International and Public Affairs at Columbia University and, since 1985, has been director of Columbia's graduate program in public policy and administration. He received his B.A. degree (1974) in political science from Franklin College and his M.A. degree (1977) and Ph.D. degree (1979) in political science from the State University of New York, Buffalo.

Cohen's main area of research and professional practice has been environmental and public management. From 1976 to 1979, he was a research fellow at the Environmental Studies Center of the State University of New York, Buffalo. From 1977 to 1978 and from 1980 to 1981, he served as policy analyst at the U.S. Environmental Protection Agency (EPA). Since leaving the EPA, Cohen has served as consultant to the Superfund hazardous-waste cleanup program, the Office of Underground Storage Tanks, and other governmental agencies. From 1984 to 1985, under contract to the EPA, he directed a major study of hazardous-waste regulation for the National Academy of Public Administration.

Cohen was assistant professor of political science at West Virginia University from 1979 to 1980 and at Columbia University from 1981 to 1985. He is the author of *The Effective Public Manager* (1988) and coauthor of *Environmental Regulation Through Strategic Planning* (1991, with S. Kamieniecki). Cohen has published a number of articles and reports on environmental policy and management issues.

Ronald Brand is former director of the Office of Underground Storage Tanks at the U.S. Environmental Protection Agency (EPA). Brand was recipient of the Presidential Rank Award (1988) in recognition of outstanding accomplishments and leadership. In 1990, he received the EPA's Gold Medal for his demonstrated leadership in TQM. He was a National Institute of Public Affairs Fellow (1965) at Princeton University's Woodrow Wilson School. Brand received his B.A. degree (1954) in public administration from New York University.

From 1978 to 1985, Brand held several managerial and policy positions at the EPA. He has also held several positions in the private sector, and from 1975 to 1978, he served as president of a management consulting firm that conducted projects in the health care management field. In Indianapolis, Indiana, he directed a nonprofit health services organization for four years. From 1958 to 1970, Brand worked in various capacities on programs of the U.S. Department of Health, Education, and Welfare, culminating in the position of deputy assistant secretary for management.

TOTAL QUALITY

MANAGEMENT

IN

GOVERNMENT

PART ONE

What Is
Total Quality Management?

CHAPTER 1

How TQM Can Strengthen
Government Performance

The senior regional program managers sit around the conference table, arguing, explaining, rationalizing, and complain-
ing about why they have, once again, failed to meet the
enforcement targets set for the year. It is now mid July, and they
have no chance of meeting their targets by the time the fiscal
year ends on September 30.

These managers argue that they have to depend on other
offices, within and outside their agency, to file enforcement
cases. A great deal of time is taken in briefings, reviews, revisions, and negotiations. Even scheduling negotiating sessions
is quite time-consuming. Since the other offices have no commitment either to the deadlines in the process or to achieving
the targets, efforts to enforce compliance with the law flounder.
This behavior has gone on for a number of years; agency heads
come and go and the problems remain the same.

In another agency, program managers are frustrated and
resigned to taking a year to award a contract for important work
that they, the Congress, and the public expect them to do. Even
with the constant addition of administrative employees, the
time to start up a new contract seems to lengthen continually,

3

and complaints, negotiations, meetings, and memos have not brought about any improvements. Fear of a mistake, which will later be caught by auditors, seems to overwhelm the system. The result is a pyramid of reviews, evasions, and questions, all intended to protect against error or the appearance of conflict. Beginning the important work needed to implement the program has taken a back seat to meeting all the rules.

In contrast, a junior program specialist observes his unit's secretaries struggling with travel authorizations, which must be prepared before anyone can take a trip. They are handwritten and then typed onto preprinted, multiple-copy forms, and if changes or errors are made, the forms must be completely redone. Tens of thousands of these travel authorizations are done each year. The analyst thinks there has to be an easier way to authorize travel. Encouraged by his recently completed total quality management (TQM) training, he decides to tackle the problem. He recognizes that many other organizations and people are involved in the process, and he creates an informal team that identifies and eliminates barriers to improving the travel authorization process over a year-long period. He works with a member of his office's management information system (MIS) group and develops a method for using the office's personal computers (PCs) and laser printers to electronically create and print the form (with all the necessary copies). They work with the agency's finance and administrative officer and get her to approve the computerized form, which is adopted for a pilot project and then later extended for use throughout the agency.

In the first cases, workers and managers at all levels complain, yell, tinker, resign, huff, and puff but never feel that they can or should attack the basic process that is creating the problem. In the third case, an employee takes a mundane but wasteful process and designs a new and better way to work. Why does this type of quality improvement occur so infrequently in complex public-sector organizations? One reason is that most employees feel that it is beyond their power to change things. A second reason is that part of the process to be improved involves people outside of their own organizational boundaries. Finally, others believe that they are so under the gun to meet pressing deadlines and deal with true emergencies that they cannot take the time to work on and improve the basic situation, whether they have ten, twenty, two hundred, or two thousand people working for them. Why do they feel this way?

Employees in the public sector are besieged on all sides with conflicting demands for productivity, quality, and service. Since many of these demands involve quotas and standards that are unrealistic and have never been attained, everyone involved is viewed as having failed. This perception of failure is shared both by those who have made the unrealistic demands and those who have attempted to respond. Bureaucrats have tried a wide variety of studies, cost-cutting measures, training, reorganizations, directives, and exhortations, but nothing has worked: government is seen as ineffectual, bloated, lazy, corrupt, and incompetent.

Any long-term observer of the public sector is bound to be cautious about claiming a solution to our government's productivity and image problems, and we share this sense of caution. TQM is not magic. It requires new knowledge, understanding of theory, sustained commitment, and a great deal of struggle to implement. If TQM is to work, an organization must accomplish a transformation of its entire working method.

Implementing Total Quality Management

Total quality management at its core includes the following simple practices:

1. Working with suppliers to ensure that the supplies utilized in the work processes are designed for your use.
2. Continuous employee analysis of work processes to improve their functioning and reduce process variation.
3. Close communication with customers to identify and understand what they want and how they define quality.

Implementing total quality management, or continuous quality improvement, is as simple as the steps described in

Exhibit 1.1. It is revolutionary because it requires management to get off its high horse and learn to work with the experts at performing work—workers on the front line. Continuous quality improvement requires a new way of managing work, in which employees are not simply ordered around but are asked to think and to participate in the process of organizing work. All members of the organization are trained in and expected to analyze work processes and to work together for improvement. The status quo is no longer worshipped. *If it is not broken, you should still try to improve it.* For example, one branch within the Office of Underground Storage Tanks at headquarters was meeting the EPA standard of responding to 100 percent of constituent mail by the established deadline. Nevertheless, they continued to search for, and found, ways to respond even faster, at the same time improving the quality of their responses by enclosing any requested materials, instead of referring the person to another information source.

Exhibit 1.1. The Operational Steps in Total Quality Management.

Step 1: Have the workers describe and measure their work and identify the work processes that should be improved, always beginning with the identification of customers and their needs.

Step 2: Describe the steps involved in performing the work. (Who does what and when?)

Step 3: Identify the places in the process that most frequently create defects, delays, and rework.

Step 4: Identify the causes of defects, delays, and rework, including poor equipment, inappropriate or unclear instructions, inadequate standard operating procedures, poor direction and communication, or inadequately trained workers and managers. Employees are often locked into a system created by management, which (since it consistently produces errors) is designed to produce errors and defects.

Step 5: Experiment with small-scale pilot projects designed to improve the process.

Step 6: If the pilot tests work, institute the changed procedure throughout the organization.

Step 7: Monitor the new process to be sure that it helps improve performance over time.

Step 8: Repeat Steps 1 through 7 and continuously improve performance.

Most large, complex organizations discourage people from analyzing their performance. Fear of failure is pervasive. However, in our review, *no news is* not *good news; it simply means that you do not know what is going on.* In the high-stress, politicized environment in which many public managers operate, no one wants to be the one to tell the boss that there is a problem.

Why should you turn to the worker as the expert? This is not out of altruism, or because you believe that *everyone* should be involved but because you need to know what only the worker knows about the real work. Have you ever watched a skilled worker install carpet, sand a floor, work at a computer, or do carpentry? You see them use methods and apply tools in ways that would never have occurred to you. They know things that you do not and cannot know without their experience and training.

The same situation exists when you are trying to solve problems or improve your operations. But where are the workers when you attempt to do this? What we usually observe is a group of managers or analysts talking at each other in a conference room, where it is frequently clear that no one knows what they are talking about. Most managers fail to respect the unique knowledge of people like the receiving clerk, the first-level grants review processor, the sanitation person who picks up the garbage, the financial analyst who reviews the budget, or the program specialist who prepares the response to an inquiry: the people who know about the barriers that keep them from doing the work right the first time.

TQM allows you to tap this source by giving employees the methods for making their knowledge and experience available. It also allows your employees to tell the truth, without fear of reprisals, to identify and share problems. It is only through a process like this that most problems can be dealt with effectively.

The well-managed organization needs to take advantage of all its brainpower, reflecting in its culture the perspective that everything can be improved, and a key organizational goal must be to identify areas that can be improved. To do this, organizations have to reorder their reward systems. Today,

people who invent a better way of doing something are rewarded, but you must also reward the person who discovers the
waste that we need to work to eliminate.

According to Deming (1986, p. 59), managers must
"drive out fear from the work place." You must build a system
that engenders an open discussion of failures as well as successes. In one regional EPA office, on first using the TQM
approach, a work group was diagramming a current procedure
on a flow chart. In describing the time that each step took, it
became apparent that the supervisor held up the work for long
periods of time. The employees could not bring themselves to
put down the actual time it took to move the action through the
boss's office (typically two weeks) and instead put down the
prescribed time (two days). It was clearly not acceptable to tell
the truth.

Why Total Quality Management Has Been Used

As American management has become professionalized, with
managers educated at business and public policy schools, the
prevailing tendency has been to ignore production line management. In the business schools, until recently we have seen a
heavy emphasis on finance and accounting. Similarly, policy
schools have emphasized high-powered quantitative analysis
and cost-benefit analysis. American universities have trained
our best minds to manipulate data and capital rather than to
understand production. In the past, with the economic pie
rapidly expanding, we could allow waste with little fear of
repercussion, so American industry and government grew fat,
complacent, and accustomed to waste. Despite these practices,
after World War II the United States was so powerful, and other
countries so weakened, that we confused our good fortune with
a distinctly effective and ingenious American management
system.

The Japanese faced a different situation after World War
II. Their industrial base had been destroyed, and unlike the
United States, they had never been blessed with abundant
natural resources. If Japanese industry was to rebuild, they

needed to find some way of applying their brainpower and human energy to the task—without the benefit of a functioning set of basic industries. Although many believe that government support and intervention were largely responsible for the renewal of Japan's industry, it succeeded, in large measure, because of a focus on improving production processes. W. Edwards Deming might have been as important to Japan's economic revival as the fabled Ministry of International Trade and Industry (MITI)—the Japanese agency that sets Japanese industrial policy. Deming taught the industrial community how to increase its competitiveness by improving the quality of the goods and services it produced. The Japanese listened because they were desperate and had little choice: the main resources intact after World War II were their energy and intelligence.

Wildly successful and powerful American industry had no motivation to learn a new way of working until relatively recently, but Japan had every motivation. Virtually starving at the end of World War II, small improvements in standards of living, and great collective sacrifice, were more generally acceptable to the average worker and to the average manager. Quality improvement requires patience and continuous, steady effort, so that instead of one big breakthrough, organizations achieve significant progress through the accumulation of hundreds of such small improvements.

The second half of the twentieth century witnessed a remarkable industrial renaissance. In the 1950s, "Made in Japan" was a joke, which meant that the product was likely to fall apart. "Made in the U.S.A." meant strength and competence. Today, although American quality continues to improve, the image of Japanese quality, particularly in automobiles and electronics, is stronger. As the world becomes a single integrated global economy, Japan's superior product and service quality in a number of areas threatens the ability of American industry to compete and therefore survive. Survival is the primary motivation behind the quality improvement movement in the United States. Ford Motor Company only came to believe that "quality is Job 1" after it learned that lesson at the hands of Honda and Toyota. If a Japanese auto factory can retool for a new model in weeks while an American factory must allocate months, it is easy to see who will have the advantage in the marketplace. American industry, forced to compete in a global marketplace, is taking a long, and at times skeptical, look at the quality management methods used by Japanese industry.

Why Government Managers Should Adopt TQM

Competition explains the appeal of TQM to industry, but what about TQM in government, the topic of this book? In the first half of the twentieth century, America's motto might well have been "the bigger the better" or "we can always get more": more labor, more natural resources, more energy, more technology. The United States grew through sheer exuberance and brawn. Two world wars ensured that America would have no real competition for world industrial dominance. Government was much the same as private industry: we thought that we could solve our problems by creating new agencies, by allowing existing bureaucracies to grow larger, and by throwing money at problems. The last decade and a half demonstrated that the old way of doing business is not sustainable. American industry is now in a life-and-death competitive struggle with an emerging global economy. If American government cannot become more productive, it will be an increasing drag on the economy, and, because of the necessity of increasing taxes, make our industry less competitive in the new global market.

The best way to improve our standard of living and the quality of the services delivered by government is to focus on the real work and free workers to make the improvements that they identify and develop. Think about it this way. The United States has an entire industry concerned with financial services to help raise and deploy capital, an entire community of scientists and engineers who work day and night to develop technological R&D breakthroughs. In government, entire staffs analyze policy issues, budgets, and information systems; however, such a staff is rarely devoted to analyzing or helping improve *how* an organization performs every aspect of its day-to-day work.

We are not advocating the creation of a "work analysis" or "quality" bureaucracy—in fact, we do not believe that the function of quality improvement should be distinguished from work itself. Thus, special organizational units to promote work analysis should probably not be created. We are arguing instead that in this era of resource scarcity one great untapped resource is every worker's knowledge and ingenuity applied to the process of performing work. Government's performance can be improved if human capital is leveraged more effectively through continuous improvement of operating processes and more efficient group processes.

The goal of improvement is to produce better and more goods and services with the same or fewer resources. Very few managers believe that they are given enough resources to do the work that they are asked to do, and, particularly in the public sector, resource limitations are expected to get worse. To begin to close the gap between resources and program needs, you must learn how to achieve more production from your present resource allocation.

Government organizations have large staffs and budgets. Even a small percentage increase in productivity can free large numbers of people and money for new tasks. For example, the United States Environmental Protection Agency (EPA) employs 18,000 people. If each person managed to eliminate twenty hours of wasted effort a year, or 1 percent of their workyear, the EPA would recover the equivalent of 180 new people. Can anyone seriously suggest that he or she did not spend twenty nonproductive hours in the last year? TQM provides an approach and tools to identify and eliminate waste of people's time, brains, and energy. Applying these concepts and tools at the EPA, for example, could mean 180 workyears to apply to different or new work needed to meet agency goals for improving and maintaining the environment.

There are other reasons to adopt TQM in government: it motivates and empowers employees, it stimulates success, and it is fun. To some degree, an organization that adopts TQM will benefit from a Hawthorne-like effect because employees will respond to the increased level of attention paid by management to improving daily operations. Furthermore, hierarchy carries with it considerable burdens. By allowing employees to become involved in designing work processes, managers can focus their attention on creatively dealing with their organization's environment and overall mission and strategy. Finally, it makes work more pleasant and fulfilling to discover the brainpower sometimes hidden in your employees.

What is in it for you? Managers who adopt TQM find that their organizations produce more. As word of your accomplishments gets around, demand for your services grows. In fact, simply making an effort to improve your organization's performance will very likely enhance your professional image. However, many of us enter the public service not to advance personally but to serve our nation and accomplish important missions. If you adopt TQM, you may well find that you are more successful in accomplishing the goals that were important to you when you entered public service.

One argument sometimes used for TQM in government is that, increasingly, government is under pressure to privatize services and contract with private firms offering lower-cost services. In this respect, it may find itself in direct competition with private firms (Osborne and Gaebler, 1992). When this occurs, the government manager may find that the organization's survival *does* depend on improved productivity and quality.

Survival, however, is only a partial argument for TQM in government. Many of government's functions are assigned because private firms are unwilling or unable to perform them. According to this argument, although private firms can collect garbage, they cannot arrest criminals. Although they can deliver mail in crowded cities, they are unlikely to find profit in delivering mail in rural Alaska. Also, private firms cannot perform government's regulatory and policy-making functions. However, private firms *can* perform elements of many tasks assigned to government. If it costs the government $11 to deliver a letter in Alaska, and Federal Express offers to deliver it for $9, even if there is no private market for the $9 letter, there might certainly be a government market for this service at this price. The government might decide to contract for this service. Therefore, the argument that TQM is needed for survival might be persuasive in an environment of cost cutting and privatization.

Having worked in and around government for a number of years, we do not believe, however, that the survival argument is the strongest one to make to public servants. People go into government in part for job security but mostly to accomplish public purposes. From the park ranger and police officer to the senior manager in the budget shop, people enter government to serve the public. Competition and, perhaps, the desire to demonstrate that government workers are as good as private sector people might provide some motivation for adopting TQM. We believe, however, that the more important argument is that TQM can help public organizations accomplish their goals.

Most people who work in government are frustrated by its poor reputation for quality and by the inefficiencies that they see and work with every day. The appeal of TQM is that it provides a method for energizing an organization and its work and improving its performance. It does not require congressional approval or a budget increase to work smarter by implementing TQM: any manager at any level can help bring it to his or her organization.

The appeal of TQM to some of the more motivated federal managers is indicated in a survey conducted by several faculty at the Kennedy School of Government at Harvard University. In a 1990 survey of seventy-two senior federal managers, Linda Kaboolian and Michael Barzaley (1990, p. 1) observed that "Total Quality Management (TQM) is achieving substantial recognition within the federal government as a way to improve organizational performance." They found that 61 percent of those surveyed had been trained in TQM and 90 percent were able to articulate TQM's core beliefs and values. They found considerable interest in TQM among these managers. On a scale ranging from 1 (not at all interested) to 4 (very interested), interest in TQM elicited an average response of 3.1 from these senior managers.

TQM Movement in Government

At the federal level, a great deal of activity is under way to encourage TQM, growing out of a general attempt throughout the 1980s to transfer private-sector management techniques to the public sector. One of the more visible initiatives to implement TQM in Washington was the establishment, in 1988, of the Federal Quality Institute by the President's Council on Management Improvement.

Quality improvement efforts in the federal government have been taking place in various offices and departments for nearly twenty years. The Department of Defense was one of the first, instituting a formal program of productivity improvement in the mid 1970s. These processes gradually evolved into a TQM approach in the mid 1980s. Additionally, the Internal Revenue Service began an organizationwide, top-down improvement campaign in 1986, which has been recognized for improvement in the quality of service to customers. Many other federal agencies have brought TQM into the workplace, including the Departments of Agriculture, Energy, Interior, and Veterans Affairs; NASA; the General Services Administration; the Environmental Protection Agency; and the Social Security Administration.

As TQM made inroads into more federal offices, many federal managers felt that a central source of information, training, and consulting services was needed. The Federal Quality Institute serves as a clearinghouse and repository, providing a focus for and stimulus to federal agencies in starting or maintaining TQM efforts. Its main functions include presenting quality awareness seminars and follow up to senior managers, maintaining information on private-sector quality consultants, and operating a resource center for federal government offices. The Institute is involved in the presentation of the Quality Improvement Prototype Award and the President's Award for Quality and has issued a series of booklets as part of the *Federal Total Quality Management Handbook.*

At the state and local level, one of the better known TQM experiments took place in Madison, Wisconsin. Joseph

Sensenbrenner, the former mayor, described his efforts to instill TQM in the operations of municipal government in a 1991 article in the *Harvard Business Review*. One of the stories he tells is a classic and bears retelling.

With city revenues constrained by falling property taxes and a high proportion of real estate owned by government and universities, Sensenbrenner turned to TQM as a means of improving the quality and efficiency of government. The first problem he attacked was the excessive amount of time required to maintain and repair vehicles at the city's garage. After making a personal appearance at the garage and demonstrating his commitment, Sensenbrenner met with line managers and local union leaders to bring them on board.

The analysis that workers conducted to improve performance at the garage was like solving a murder mystery. As a result of talking to the mechanics about the repair process, Sensenbrenner's analysis team determined that many of the delays involved waiting for proper spare parts to come in, because they were not all kept in stock. Taking this information to the parts department manager, the team was told that it was impossible to maintain an adequate stock of parts because the city fleet had so many different types, makes, models, and model years of equipment. Inquiring further, the team found that the city's purchasing policy required it to buy the vehicle or piece of equipment that had the lowest price on the purchase date and met the procurement specifications.

From the results of this kind of short-sighted policy, it was obvious that the city was not saving money. But was there a way to change it? The parts department manager suggested that delays would be reduced if fewer models were purchased— parts could then be stored in bulk. However, the manager added, central purchasing would not allow the change in policy.

Continuing up the ladder to central purchasing, the analysis team explained what they had found out and asked what could be done. Central purchasing told them that it was a good idea and they would certainly agree to it, but the city comptroller would not approve revisions in the purchasing requirements. Moving on to the city comptroller's office, the analysis team again presented its findings. The city comptroller agreed that the proposal would save money but said that the city attorney would not allow it. In the city attorney's office, the analysis team was told that it was a simple process to revise the purchasing requirements to identify ease of maintenance as a priority when writing up the specifications. After making revisions to the purchasing requirements, Sensenbrenner's analysis team tracked improvements. Average downtime for repairs and maintenance was reduced by two-thirds, and the city was saving about $700,000 per year.

Looking back on this project, Sensenbrenner identified three elements that he describes as instrumental to understanding the success. The first was realizing that "the source of the downtime problem was upstream in the relationship of the city to its suppliers—not downstream where the worker couldn't find a missing part. The problem was a flawed system, not flawed workers" (Sensenbrenner, 1991, p. 68). Although the answer was simple, it was not obvious. A great deal of investigation and sleuthing by the team was necessary to understand what was really going on, but it paid off in the end.

Second, teamwork among a number of self-contained departments was essential to solving the problem. The real success of TQM includes not only solving problems like these but also using methods that break down barriers to communication so that the problems do not have the opportunity to arise.

Finally, developing a real solution meant that management had to get participation from frontline employees (the ones who work directly with the process itself) and not just focus on the results. Without their inputs, a "solution" could have been imposed from above—such as telling the parts manager to simply order more parts—but that would not have addressed the structural factors that caused the problem, and it would have created additional difficulties.

How will TQM change the way that you manage and work in government? TQM leads us to constantly improve work systems—the standard procedures that we follow to complete work. It asks that we look at our work as an element of a system with inputs (supplies), outputs (programs), and outcomes (customer satisfaction). The "we" who look at work or analyze work are composed of not just management and not just consultants but everyone, including the people who do the work, customers and suppliers.

CHAPTER 2

The Basic Concepts
of TQM

This chapter discusses in detail the essential core concepts of total quality management. In our view these can be reduced to three key elements:

1. Working with suppliers to ensure that the supplies utilized in the work processes are designed for your use.
2. Continuous employee analysis of work processes to improve their functioning and reduce process variation.
3. Close communication with customers to identify and understand what they want and how they define quality.

Core Concept Number 1: Working with Suppliers

Work processes do not exist in isolation. If your organization is to perform its tasks, it requires certain supplies. A central feature of TQM is the concept of an interactive work process, in which the worker takes a supply and adds value to it to make it fit for use by a customer. TQM requires constant analysis of customer needs (see below). However, once you know what your customers need, you must remember that you are also someone else's customer—you are your supplier's customer. Since your suppliers may not be adherents of TQM, you may need to be proactive and speak to them directly about your needs. Often, your suppliers are your outside contractors or consultants; sometimes, however, they are your organization's print shops, personnel offices, and general counsel offices.

If you speak to them before they produce the product they are supplying you with, you can often get them to alter their product design. Whether it is the format of the data that they are giving you or a standard operating procedure that they are following out of habit, a better supply can sometimes be obtained, without much struggle, after a simple phone call or a short meeting. Sometimes it is a more difficult process, but by investing time in discussions with your suppliers you can often reduce the amount of work you must perform to produce what your customers need. Sometimes you do not reduce your workload but instead produce a product of higher quality because you are starting with a more appropriate, higher-quality supply. Exhibit 2.1 is a Supplier Analysis Worksheet that

Exhibit 2.1. Supplier Analysis Worksheet.

Take your current project and identify the suppliers for that project on the grid below. Then analyze what you need from these suppliers. Are you getting what you need? How might you stimulate improved performance from your suppliers?

	Suppliers	
	Who Are They?	What Do You Need from Them?
Internal		
External		

enables you to list your internal and external suppliers and identify what you need from them in order to produce a specific product.

Core Concept Number 2: Continuous Staff Analysis of Work Processes

Supplier communication is critical for improving work processes, although it is often not the starting point. Often, the starting point is an analysis of the organization's current level of performance. This is an ongoing process. As we discuss the core concept of continuous analysis of work processes, we will focus on four issues: (1) the rationale for continuous improvement, (2) the importance of worker participation in analyzing work processes, (3) amnesty: making it possible to tell management the truth, and (4) improving productivity by analyzing and improving quality.

Rationale for Continuous Improvement

Most workers and managers work away at their jobs and only occasionally come up with an improvement that is adopted by the organization. These improvements are sometimes rewarded with an outstanding performance rating or even a bonus; then everyone goes back to work with the new routine established and waits for the muse to visit again. Certainly that was the way work was done in the dozen or so government organizations that we both worked with over the years.

When Ronald Brand went through his first TQM training, he was handed a badge that said, "My job: continuous improvement in quality and productivity." James Copley of Conway Quality, the trainer at this session, kept adding the word "forever" to the credo on the badge, emphasizing it throughout the training. It was unsettling, since we were used to celebrating and resting up after each improvement.

How does one understand and seek continuous improvement? The best example of this is the work of Shigeo Shingo. Brand attended a conference in Indianapolis in March 1990, in which 750 workers and managers from around the country participated. Its focus was SMED, or "single minute exchange of die." For three days, individuals and teams from different companies explained and showed slides, videos, and demonstrations of how they improved the process of production changeover. They described how they cut the time it took to change over a factory's machines and processes from thirty-eight hours to less than ten minutes. Obviously, a longer changeover period means a longer downtime, which is undesirable, since nothing is being produced. Naturally, such downtime must be seen as a form of waste—or at least a form of necessary work that does not directly contribute to the welfare of a customer.

What Brand learned from these teams and from listening to Shingo and reading Taichi Ohno of Toyota was that their improvements of thousands of percent were not achieved by investments of millions of dollars in capital improvements. Instead, they consisted of hundreds of small improvements identified by the workers in a focused daily and weekly effort. (An example is substituting a one-turn locking and unlocking handle for screwing in and unscrewing eighteen screws to attach or release a plate.) Most important, it was clear that none of these teams felt that their drive to improve production processes was over. Each was still excited about shaving additional seconds and minutes off their processes.

Brand was kidded by the attendees in Indianapolis because he was the only government person in attendance. "What are you doing here?" they would ask. He would respond, "You are going from hours to minutes, and we are trying to go from months to weeks or days on our processes."

We have seen these ideas applied to government activities. For example, travel authorizations are necessary work that do not directly add to the welfare of any government clients. As discussed earlier, one staffer at the EPA came up with an improved way to do these authorizations, which saves over ten minutes per transaction. There are over 200,000 of these travel "widgets" processed a year on our assembly line, so this savings translates to about sixteen full time equivalents (FTEs)

(10 x 200,000 saves 33,333 workhours, or about sixteen FTEs if we assume a workyear of about 2,100 hours). If we could eliminate many of the small wasteful processes that vacuum time out of our workday, we would be assured of finding similar opportunities for savings. Imagine all of the increased service we could provide or reduced costs we might uncover this way.

An enforcement group in the EPA's Philadelphia regional office was concerned about the time it took between the identification of a violator of water pollution requirements and the issuance of a notice of violation (NOV). A team of engineers and lawyers worked on reducing the EPA's response time. They simplified the process by spelling out the review criteria in advance and by creating standard clauses used for particular types of violations. The first phase of the project reduced the time for issuing NOVs from fifty-nine days to six days. Most important, the team has not stopped looking for additional improvements.

Importance of Worker Participation in Analysis

One of the most important differences between TQM and traditional notions of production analysis and improvement is the issue of who does the analysis. Under TQM, the worker is the expert at analyzing and identifying obstacles to improving work processes. In the early days of scientific production management, assembly lines such as the one constructed at the Ford Motor Company were built on extensive analyses of work processes. These time-motion studies and other efforts at production analysis broke down production activities into their most minute elements. Since workers were considered merely interchangeable extensions of machines, they were not seen as capable of participating in work analysis. The idea of workers conducting analyses of their own tasks in fact seemed vaguely subversive. Work analysis was seen as (and was) antilabor and antihuman when it was conducted by the stereotypical guy with the stopwatch and clipboard. These analyses often misdiagnosed problems and proposed impractical solutions, and also, they were frequently not implemented due to lack of credibility with foremen and workers on the line. This is not to say that the rationalization of work and mass production did not result in tremendous advances in productivity. Rather, we would argue that such an analysis eventually reaches a point of diminishing returns. Unless the worker lends his or her expertise and energy to the enterprise, further increases in productivity will be very difficult to obtain.

Worker self-analysis should *not* be confused with worker democracy. Worker self-analysis is exactly that; workers analyze their own work processes and try to improve them. Worker democracy is an entirely different concept and has its roots in the same social forces that created representative democracy. Workplace democracy can mean either of two things: (1) participation by all employees for the purpose of controlling organizational direction and outputs or (2) participation with the goal of influencing conditions in the workplace. In the United States, the idea of worker participation to control government direction is problematic since administration is supposed to reflect the instructions of democratically elected political officials (Cohen, 1992).

Worker self-analysis, however, results in suggestions to management about the way work processes should be organized and conducted. Management must decide whether to use these suggestions. Naturally, if management encourages suggestions but rarely uses them, eventually the number of suggestions will significantly diminish. Self-analysis does not mean that workers are unassisted in conducting or presenting analyses; they may need help from statisticians, engineers, management consultants, and a host of other experts.

We are not arguing that employees will, in all cases, be ingenious at developing improved work processes. Sometimes your employees will not be capable of such creativity—although our experience has been that self-analysis unleashes tremendous creative energy in most work settings. Rather, we are arguing that people involved in performing work are always the most expert at identifying problems and obstacles in completing the work. They can typically describe the work process at a level of detail that is far more specific than that of a manager. This is to be expected: these tasks are a major part of their day-to-day experience, and they should know them better than their manager does. This intimate knowledge of the work process is the new information brought to bear on production analysis by TQM.

Worker self-analysis has a number of critical advantages. First, it encourages workers to bring their brains to the office and not "check them at the door." This can encourage creativity, increase morale, and result in a greater commitment to the organization and to the task at hand. More important, we believe that the people who do the work know more about how it is conducted than any "expert" who observes work as a consultant or analyst. You may believe that you understand why your secretary cannot get memos produced on time, but you are not the one who deals with broken laser printers, phone interruptions, lines at the copier, and a boss too busy to approve the final draft in a timely manner.

With a little encouragement, your employees can become spectacular diagnosticians of work processes. Nothing is more motivating than taking a task that you find frustrating and figuring out a faster, less error-prone way of doing it. Furthermore, if employees are trained to analyze their own work and are allowed to implement improvement that they design, the odds are high that the improvement will actually be adopted. If the employees own these new work processes, they take pride in the improvement and work hard to make the new system, *their* new system, work. Sometimes the new process itself is not appreciably better than the old one but will produce a self-created Hawthorne effect.

Another important factor about worker self-analysis is that the employees do not conduct work analyses individually but as part of quality improvement teams. These teams include other employees working in the same area and may also include subject matter experts and/or a facilitator expert in the techniques of TQM analysis. Often, these groups stimulate creative problem solving that individuals working alone could not accomplish. The improvement teams can also enhance communication among employees from different parts of the organization and help build identification with the organization's mission.

There is a misconception that TQM can only be used on factory production lines. In fact, quality improvement teams can be particularly useful in administrative settings, both in and out of government. Unlike many factory workers, white-collar employees are used to performing analytical work. The main problem that they have with TQM analysis is that they are used to aiming their analytical guns at others. They have focused their brainpower on analyzing everything *except* the way that they perform their own tasks, although they certainly know their own work better than anyone else and therefore are the "experts" at performing that work.

Amnesty: Making It Possible to Tell Management the Truth

Amnesty requires both employees and management to perform the difficult task of separating people from the problem. We define amnesty as an aspect of an organization's culture, actively instituted and reinforced by management to reward truth-telling about work processes. Not only are employees not punished for expressing their views but they are rewarded for making the effort. Amnesty does not mean that employees are free to personally insult managers or fellow employees—it is not an invitation to declare open season for nasty dialogue. It also does not mean that management is forbidden to criticize employee performance. It means, in Deming's terms, "drive out fear." Management provides mechanisms and incentives to encourage honest discussion of how work gets done; management listens and does not label various employee voices as belonging to "friends" or "foes."

Workers may be expert at performing their own tasks, but management controls the resources and authority needed to implement improvements in work processes. It is not enough, then, for employees to analyze work; at least some of the improvements they identify and suggest must then be implemented. Since workers must be authorized by management to implement these improvements, active and honest communication between employees and management is an essential element of total quality management.

Most of the work processes that are in place in an organization have been established by management. Employees can be very reluctant to criticize those processes if they believe they will be subjected to reprisals for voicing their views. It is human nature to prefer good news to bad news. Employees in bureaucratic organizations learn early on that there is little to be gained by being the bearer of bad news, and often, the messenger becomes identified with the message.

We have found this aspect of TQM a particularly difficult one to put into effect. In governmental bureaucracies concepts of hierarchy are particularly ingrained, and it is difficult to change patterns of behavior to create an environment of amnesty. Managers are used to deference and often do not want to be subjected to rigorous analysis of how work is organized and performed in their units. Rather than describing current levels of performance and diagnosing causes and effects, we often see a fair amount of personal criticism and efforts to assign blame for poor performance. Even trained policy analysts are not in the habit of thinking analytically about their own work processes. Their ego and sense of self-worth may be threatened by any effort to be honest about how work gets done. The way to overcome this problem is simply to keep working at it. Management must insist on honesty but must also insist on good human relations—a certain gentleness and compassion to accompany "ruthless" truth-telling.

There is another, more serious problem with amnesty in a governmental setting. Government bureaucracies operate in a fishbowl (Cohen, 1988). An honest self-appraisal of an organization's current level of performance can be leaked to those outside the agency and become a public relations nightmare. At one point, we conducted an aggressive internal reexamination of the federal tank regulatory program and its work processes. Every person in the organization participated in a series of small-group interviews and frankly discussed the organization's accomplishments and problems. Notes on these meetings were written and circulated to employees for their comments. Halfway through this process we realized that as useful as these written notes were to a frank self-assessment, they could be easily misunderstood if they were leaked to the press. Our advice on this issue is to note that self-criticism in government must be done in a manner that helps ensure confidentiality. Otherwise, people will not feel free to tell the truth about problems and their causes. We would advise against *circulating* copious notes on your organization's problems. As much as possible, the critique should be communicated orally and kept within the organization.

TQM will not be credible to your staff if amnesty is not real; workers will quickly test to see if amnesty is truly going to prevail. This happened early on in the EPA's Office of Underground Storage Tanks. A few weeks after their first TQM training, three workers asked to meet with the OUST management team. At the meeting, they explained that they had done a study of the office's accountability system, applying the TQM concepts they had learned. The system called for everyone to plan projects for their work for the year: analyses, regulatory studies, field tests, or development of guidance, manuals, or videos. Each project leader and team member created project milestones that were entered into the computer and reported progress against these milestones weekly. Every Monday, the management team met to review progress and to prod or assist project leaders as necessary. There were about eighty projects in the listing.

Displaying hand-drawn data on flip charts, the self-created TQM team proceeded to demonstrate the following:

1. The office met its scheduled milestones 10 percent of the time.
2. In the weekly meetings the management team did not provide assistance but simply demanded that the project managers do better (without helping them figure out how to do better).
3. Entering data into the accountability system and running the entire process took about one and one-half workyears, or about 4 percent of our total workforce.
4. There was no value added for our customers, our workers, or management from this process.

After the presentation, OUST management decided, on the spot, that the accountability system was pure waste and should be eliminated, although some people felt that the system should not be dropped until a replacement was designed. Later, a team did come up with a much simpler, more focused process that took about one-tenth of the effort.

The point here is that this incident sent the signal that there was amnesty, that the sacred cows could be questioned, that the messenger would not be killed, and that action could be taken quickly. This test comes up in a variety of forms as organizations undertake the TQM journey. We suggest you be prepared for it and be sure to send the right signals.

Improving Productivity by Analyzing and Improving Quality

When Steven Cohen teaches TQM to public administration students, he often introduces this concept by telling the story of two cars he has purchased: an American car in the 1970s and a Japanese car in the 1980s. In 1975, he bought a Plymouth Duster when he was in graduate school in Buffalo. Before he drove the car off the lot, the salesman advised him to keep a pad and pen on the front seat over the next month and list anything wrong with the car. The salesman assured Steven that Chrysler stood behind its products and any defects would be repaired or replaced free of charge. Over the next month, the pad gradually became filled with about two dozen minor (at least not life-threatening) defects: the turn signal would not lock in place for right turns, the glove compartment kept flying open, the passenger window rattled, and so on. True to his word, the dealer fixed all of the small defects, and after the 1,000-mile checkup the car was in good repair.

In 1983, Steven was working as a consultant for the federal nuclear waste program in a suburb of Washington, D.C., and decided to buy a new car. He bought a Honda Accord from a dealer in Rockville, Maryland. As he got ready to drive the car off the lot, he asked the salesman if he should keep a pad on the front seat and list the defects for the 1,000-mile checkup. The salesman gave Cohen a horrified look and said, "Defects? List? No. Please, let me explain, you've bought a Honda—there should be no defects. If you find anything wrong with the car at any moment—call me immediately. Here is my work number and here is my home phone number." Naturally, this being a car dealer and Steve being a New Yorker, he was a little suspicious. After receiving assurances that the dealer would, in fact, fix anything that might be wrong with the car, he drove off. Weeks went by, and the car worked perfectly.

What was the difference? In neither case was he driving a handcrafted Rolls Royce. Both cars were mass-produced. But in the case of the Honda, quality was built into the production process and defects were eliminated before the car reached the customer. Our guess is that the car salesman could give out his home number without fear of frequent phone calls. In the case of the 1975 Chrysler, the customer was the quality control inspector. The car was shipped with the assumption—held even by the salesperson and workers—that the car would have more defects than the driver could remember without notes. This was evidence of enormous waste in the production process and a failure, on the part of management, to emphasize and reward defect prevention. In the rush to ship products and meet production targets, cars were shipped before they were really ready. Workers on the line almost certainly knew they were making a car with defects. However, rather than analyzing the cause of those defects and attempting to eliminate them, the workers did the best they could and moved the car down the line to the next station. Quality control at the end of the line removed most of the more defective vehicles and those that got by would be "inspected" by the dealer or the customer.

The result of ignoring quality and not building it into the production process is an overall decline in productivity. Wasted parts and labor and extensive warranty work may seem to be inevitable elements in a modern mass-production process, but they need not be. In fact, TQM demonstrates that the time invested in improving production processes and reducing defects more than pays for itself in reduced waste and reduced levels of rework. In addition, allowing the customer to play the role of product user rather than quality control inspector dramatically increases satisfaction.

In administrative processes a similar phenomenon can be observed. By paying attention to how you produce regulations and forms and how you exchange information, you can improve production processes and reduce errors, redrafts, and information disconnects. You must invest in the time it takes to analyze production processes, but there is so much waste in administrative processes that you can easily and quickly recoup your investment. This improved level of quality in the work that you do can quickly and dramatically improve your productivity. The waste takes many forms and can include delays resulting from poor instructions, rework, callbacks, and constant calls for clarifications.

The key to understanding this concept is to get beyond the association of quality with craft. There is an assumption that mass production and administration of services, in some fashion, inherently involve a trade-off between quantity and quality, which is why improving productivity by improving quality seems so counterintuitive. When employees analyze work processes, however, they should do so not with the goal of making the product more quickly or cheaply but of making the service produced better.

Core Concept Number 3: Working with Your Customer

If the goal of TQM is to continuously improve quality, we must have some way of defining what quality is.

Customer Decides Quality

We define quality as the degree to which a product or service is valued by a customer and fit for use. Central to this definition are the perceptions, values, and beliefs of customers. People in government often have difficulty with the notion that the quality of their work is ultimately judged by a customer. However, there is little question that if work is to generate the resources needed for an organization to survive, it must be done for the customer. Deming in his *Out of the Crisis* says that there is a difference between most service and manufacturing jobs: "An important difference is that a production worker in manufacturing not only has a job: he is aware that he is doing his part to make something that somebody will see, feel and use in some way . . . he has some idea about the quality of the final product. In contrast, in many service organizations, the people that work there only have a job. They are not aware that they have a product, and that this product is service; that good service and happy customers keep his company in business and provide jobs; that an unhappy customer may bring loss of business and of his job" (1986, p. 188).

How can you lose business in a public-sector organization? Most managers do not really think about this issue but tend to think of government as a monopoly, with an inexhaustible supply of captive customers. On the other hand, most managers have seen agencies denied resources and personnel or bypassed on work and decisions. Some examples follow:

1. When people perceive no value added from your organization, they do not take your advice or admonitions seriously. This frequently creates redoing work.
2. People try to circumvent your office. Think, for example, of the training, budget, personnel, and public information offices in your agency. Do you ever attempt to avoid them in your effort to complete projects?
3. Good candidates are not sent or recommended for jobs in your office.
4. Others do not support additional dollars, employees, space, or equipment for your organization because they assume that your organization does not contribute value to the larger organization or purpose.
5. People in intern and job-rotation programs do not select your office as an assignment, thus depriving it of new ideas and free help and also robbing it of a chance to influence people who will work elsewhere in the organization and may be your future suppliers.
6. People resort to use of contractors and consultants to help them when they could have called on you for assistance.

Too often, managers and employees decide that they know what the customer needs and wants. Unfortunately, the failure to consult customers is probably the most common cause of customer dissatisfaction: managers and employees must find out who their customers are and what they need. This can be done in a variety of valid ways: surveys, focus groups, calls or visits to users and nonusers of your product or service, and feedback from field personnel.

In evaluating customer needs, it is very important to listen carefully. For example, in the tank regulation program, the Office of Underground Storage Tanks (OUST) wanted tank owners and operators to test their tanks to see if they were leaking. The EPA issued a regulation requiring them to test their tanks by a certain deadline. However, in discussions with these customers, OUST found that even those who wanted to comply needed help from us. Tank owners wanted help in selecting a company and method for testing their tanks. Companies that provided testing services needed help to convince tank owners that they were required by law to test their tanks. Once OUST understood this, the organization worked to develop products, guides, and videos in order to help meet their needs.

All of these extra steps were important if the EPA was to successfully carry out its program. OUST needed to push, prod, and otherwise convince tank owners to make the decision to test the nearly two million tanks in operation; the organization needed vendors to build or expand businesses and invest money to supply the testing services. This was all necessary to meet the needs of 700,000 tank owners and operators. Since the EPA wanted them to comply voluntarily, we decided to think of them as customers and help them in any way possible so that we could achieve our environmental goals.

Three additional examples further illustrate the problem of identifying customers of government programs.

Defining Customers of the IRS. Al Kolak, special assistant to the commissioner of the Internal Revenue Service, once observed: "We never thought of taxpayers as being our customers." Kolak explained that taxpayers generally fall into three categories: (1) those who want to comply and therefore file their taxes correctly and on time, (2) those who want to comply but do not know how to file their returns and therefore make errors, and (3) those who do not want to comply and either intentionally falsify or omit information or simply do not file their returns at all.

Kolak noted that before implementing TQM in his office, "We behaved as if everyone was in the third category." Such a perception was hardly conducive to viewing the taxpayers as customers of the IRS.

How does defining the customer, and hence changing your perception of the relationship between you and the customer, alter the methods of work? As in the case of the IRS, you start by analyzing the mistakes that cause rework, rather than assuming that the taxpayer is to blame for the errors. This analysis leads you to find and eliminate the cause of the mistakes, rather than accepting the additional rework.

Customer Analysis at the Department of the Treasury. An example of this analysis can be found at the U.S. Treasury in the unit that processes claims from individuals who have lost their savings bond certificates. There are over 75,000 such cases a year. At one point, almost half of these claims were being submitted with incomplete or inaccurate information and had to be redone. Until the employees of the processing unit recognized that almost 50 percent of their work was actually rework, they simply accepted the demanding workload. It was only when they identified the bond owner as their customer, and thus began to analyze the relationship between them and their customer, that they could take a new approach to their work.

Let us imagine, for example, that a bond owner has lost her bond certificate, and she is worried because she will need to cash in the bond to cover school expenses. To request a new certificate, she completes the form provided by the Treasury. Under the circumstances, does she wish to provide less than complete information? No. Does she want a quick response? Of course.

After analyzing this and other scenarios, the workers in the processing unit attempted to determine the best way to meet the needs of the bond owners, their customers. They gathered data on and examined the forms, process, and instructions to see how they could be revised to make errors and omissions less likely. By asking these questions, the employees began to improve the process.

These two examples illustrate how the processes in the work environment can be improved by identifying the customer. Rather than placing blame and accepting rework as inevitable, it is possible to analyze ways of improving the work flow between the customer and your organization. Failing to specifically identify the customer is a problem that occurs more often than not. Frequently, public-sector agencies claim: "Everyone is our customer," or "The taxpayers are our customers." Perhaps in the long run this is true, but such a universal definition does not prove helpful in trying to make the many choices that workers, supervisors, managers, and elected officials have to make.

When Brand served as a member of the board of directors of a hospital in Indiana, he quickly learned that if he wanted to serve the hospital's patients and the community at large, he had a primary customer to serve first. That customer was the physician. Most patients come to a hospital because of their physician. This is not to say that in a system of production such as a hospital there are not a variety of potential customers and a vast network of supplier-customer relationships, including physicians, administrators, nurses, laboratory technicians, maintenance crews, cafeteria workers, and patients. However, without physicians there are no patients and without patients, all of those support jobs disappear.

Customer Analysis at the EPA's Office of Underground Storage Tanks (OUST). OUST recognized that citizens near leaking tank sites were concerned about air pollution emitted during cleanups. This made air emissions a key issue for the program's major clients—not the broad public, but the state environmental staff responsible for managing the cleanup operation. The state inspection team needed to know whether gasoline vapors were escaping from soils that were excavated from a tank site, which were piled alongside the excavation. One OUST staffer worked with contractors to develop a simple method for calculating these emissions, which was included in a brief manual and sent out to state field personnel for comment. One comment bears retelling: "We took your method and tested it in the field. It works. This is the best thing you guys have done."

Clearly, OUST understood that the customers would eventually decide on a definition of quality, despite the project team's effort to talk with customers and determine their needs in the design stage of the method and manual. Feedback from the field would tell whether the team had met its goal of assisting field personnel to make better and faster decisions about soil vapors.

This success contrasts with another earlier project that OUST undertook to help these same customers. A project team worked with state field personnel to develop a manual to help them conduct thorough assessments of places where a pollution release was detected or suspected. The team sent drafts of the manual out to the EPA regional offices and some states and made many revisions, cranking out new versions. Brand suspected that the team was trying to do too many things with a single tool, the manual. Finally, OUST sent it out as a finished product, but the project team never heard a word from the program's regional or state customers. If quality is defined as meeting customer requirements, then something was terribly wrong. How could the project team have labored so long and failed to serve the program's customers? Once again the customer had decided what quality was, and OUST was not providing it.

Brand found that he had to constantly fight deeply ingrained standard operating procedures and fear of new practices. A typical government agency approach is to look at a problem, decide on the best way to handle it, and then prescribe or teach that approach as the only true and right way to do the job. Once that method is adopted in the field it is very difficult to change, the situation becomes quite static, and improvement is difficult to stimulate. For example, one OUST quality improvement team found that field measurements could be used to assess the conditions at a contaminated site.

This method is faster and less expensive than gathering samples and sending them to a laboratory for analysis and, most important, it permits corrective action to start sooner, thereby limiting the spread of pollution. One barrier to implementing these techniques was that state and local field personnel were not sure of how to conduct and interpret the field measurements. Since they were concerned about this, they fell back to using laboratory analyses, frankly admitting that they did this to "cover our rear."

To overcome this discomfort level, OUST decided to develop and carry out training for the field inspectors. One decision made the breakthrough that helped us meet customers' requirements for quality training. Each inspector was asked to bring his or her own field measurement equipment to the training courses, which were called "vapor survey boot camps." Instead of being forced to learn with the typical or best or newest equipment, they learned practical ways to apply their own equipment. This made a tremendous difference in learning, comfort, and the likelihood that their training would be implemented on the job. The team had worked hard to design a quality training experience, but the trainees, and ultimately their use of the training, would determine whether the training program met or exceeded their requirements.

A test you can apply is to look at a project in your office or agency that has been going on for some time. Sit down with your staff and spend a few hours discussing who the customer is. What will develop, in a sample federal agency, is this sort of chain:

Who	*Customer*
Worker	Worker's boss
Supervisor	Budget office, legal counsel, a payroll processing unit, supervisor's boss
Branch chief	Schedule and accountability system, division chief
Division chief	Agency head, outside groups: industry or public interest

	groups, a congressional staffer, Office of Management and Budget
Bureau chief, agency head	Congress, press, White House, key outside group leaders

Often, however, this does not play out so easily. The development of a regulation, for example, can take two or three years. It can involve work groups that include regional, state, industry, and public representatives, as well as a variety of headquarters staff who meet, discuss, argue, prepare issue papers, and hold briefings. Yet they rarely, if ever, discuss the issue of who their customers are. They rarely ask themselves about whom they are trying to satisfy and whose requirements and expectations they are trying to meet.

In fact, the concept of *customer* is alien to many government agencies. More often than not, the public official defines his or her role as pursuing better housing or education or health care. Such attitudes often underlie the dangerous belief that the official will make choices without consideration of the people who are affected by the choice because they are "not objective or sophisticated enough to understand why it has to be this way."

Projecting and Diagnosing Customer Demands

When thinking about customers and the programs or services they want produced, it is important to understand that customer communication can be tricky. Customers do not always explicitly express their demands. One can satisfy a customer's demands by giving them what they ask for, but sometimes they do not ask for things that they expect, so you must project these expectations. For example, when you make reservations for a hotel room, you do not ask, "Do you provide clean sheets?" You expect them. But if you do not get clean sheets, you are very dissatisfied. That is the key thing about expectations: people only notice them when they are not met.

Let us look at some expectations of government agencies. The public expects that responses to public telephone inquiries will be polite. When a memo notes that an item is attached, the reader should find the enclosed item. Also, people expect that technical, legal, and financial issues will be explained so that nonspecialists can understand them. The public expects that when they dial 911, an emergency vehicle will arrive promptly. When they turn on the spigot, they expect that reasonably clean water will appear. No one has explicitly articulated these demands, but the minute they are not met, customers are dissatisfied.

One indicator that customer analysis has reached a sophisticated level in an organization is when customer expectations are routinely exceeded. We believe that there is hardly any product or service for which you cannot find some way to exceed expectations. Two recent examples from Ronald Brand's personal experience will illustrate this.

Brand recently purchased an Amana refrigerator. Enclosed with the operating instructions and warranty was a single page titled "The Sounds of Your Refrigerator." On it was a picture of the refrigerator with ten arrows pointing to different parts of the refrigerator. Each arrow pointed to a different type of sound and explained the sound and its cause. When these sounds occurred, he looked at the chart, was able to identify the cause, and did not have to worry. The company benefited because he did not telephone for help or create a service call under warranty. That single page, creatively executed, gave him a secure feeling and exceeded his expectations.

Brand's second example has to do with buying season tickets for the basketball games at the University of Richmond. When Brand called to purchase season tickets, the agent asked where he lived and suggested that since he was close by, he would probably be able to make a better choice of seat selections if he stopped by the arena. Brand agreed and went right over. The ticket agent provided a seating chart and Brand selected two seats from those available. Then the agent said, "Would you like to see the location you will be sitting in?" He then came out of his ticket booth and took Brand into the arena, where Brand went to the seats he had selected and sat in them. The agent pointed out where the band would be and the home-team bench. Finally, when he prepared the tickets he asked if Brand was eligible for the senior citizen discount. Brand did not realize they had such a benefit. Thanks to the ticket agent, the tickets ended up costing one-half the regular price. That ticket agent certainly understood how to exceed expectations.

Analyzing Customer Needs

To know what tasks to perform, you must have an understanding of your customer's needs. The term *customer* is sometimes alien to those in the public sector; some prefer the term *client*. We define customer as the people who use the things that you produce. If you write a memo for your boss, your boss is your customer. If you write a regulation governing a private firm's behavior, you have a number of customers. The first stage in communicating with your customers is to identify who they are. We think it is helpful for you to divide your customers into two groups, internal (those who work inside your organization) and external (those who work outside your organization). Along with our consultants, Tom Ingersoll and Gardner Shaw, we designed a simple worksheet that you can use when conducting a customer analysis (see Exhibit 2.2).

To use this sheet, take a specific project or process that you are involved in and list those people or organizations inside and outside your agency that will use what you produce. Then attempt to find out what their expectations are. It is possible that various customers want different and apparently incompatible things. Sometimes you can devise a solution that will meet diverse needs; however, it may be impossible to design a single product that will satisfy all of your customers. You really have three choices when faced with conflicting or divergent customer needs: (1) abandon one customer in order to appeal to another, (2) attempt to change your customer's preferences, or (3) design a "compromise" product that provides less than each customer would consider optimal but enough to satisfy both.

Exhibit 2.2. Customer Analysis Worksheet.

Take your current project and identify the customers for that project on the grid below. Then analyze your customer's needs.

Customers

	Who Are They?	What Do They Need from You?
Internal		
External		

In the public sector, it is often difficult to explicitly abandon a customer; certainly it is often unwise to make a public announcement of your decision to give up on some clientele. Often you will need to pursue option two or three. The point we are making is that you should not begin the process of designing a product or program until you have identified your customers and analyzed their needs.

Analyzing customer needs requires that you talk with and listen to your customers as much as you can. You need to ask enough questions and communicate sufficiently with them in order to know what they want. How many times have you had to redo a project because you did not understand what your boss needed, or because your boss did not understand what he or she wanted? It is easy to ignore the issue of learning about the needs of your external customers. This is particularly true of federal and state governments that may be somewhat removed from the direct delivery of services. Sometimes the feedback loops are quite attenuated. However, it is critical that you get out from behind your desks and get on the road or on the phone and talk to the people outside your building who rely on the products, services, or programs that your organization delivers.

CHAPTER 3

How TQM Revolutionizes Management

What did the EPA face in implementing the Underground Storage Tank program? There were fifty separate state programs to regulate underground oil and chemical storage tanks and to clean up leaks from those tanks. In some states, the portion of the program designed to prevent tank leaks was housed in one agency and the leak cleanup work in another. In some states, the fire marshall's office conducted inspections and collected fees while the environmental agency in the state assessed sites with gasoline releases and conducted or oversaw corrective action operations. Each state had different laws, practices, budget processes, procurement standards, and hiring rules. Some had district offices, some were run centrally, and some delegated work to local governments.

Although underground tank programs were under way, they varied greatly. How would the EPA ensure their adequacy, quality, and responsiveness? Based on his experiences in government where he had seen traditional tools used with little if any resulting change in program performance, Brand felt that these tools of oversight, audit reports, and written directives were inadequate. Brand liked to refer to the program as a series of assembly lines, but this was not true operationally. For example, over 200,000 tanks were closed and removed. Each had to go through a common series of steps: notification, vapor purging, removal, and assessment of the site for contamination and corrective action, if necessary. However, this process occurred in fifty different organizations (the states) and sometimes in different city or county agencies, each of which varied in some respect.

OUST had tried, over time, to introduce improvements in the assembly lines by developing improved tools and methods and disseminating them to the states. OUST worked with the states to analyze work processes and develop ways to improve them, but actual adoption and implementation was nonexistent or occurred in only one or two locations a year. Senior management worried about being accountable to the EPA's administrator and especially Congress for the performance of the national program. The OUST employees at both headquarters and the regions grew increasingly frustrated.

Management as Facilitating Improvement

As the organization learned more about TQM, and as the staff learned about the differences among state programs, it became clear that each state needed to progress from its particular current level of performance. For example, the first stage in cleaning up a leak from an underground tank is to develop a plan for assessing the environmental conditions at a particular site. If one state takes thirty days to approve a site assessment plan so that work can start, and another state does not require plans to be submitted at all, different approaches to improvement need to be taken. Many of the state requirements, practices, and procedures were driven by state-specific history and values. Only by helping state workers and managers make improvements within their organizations and political environments could the program succeed. The states knew what their real work was, and their ideas and expertise were essential to the development of a high-quality national program. OUST needed many states to work at thinking up and making continuous improvements, which, cumulatively, would make for a continuously improving and successful national program.

Providing training in TQM to the states was OUST's major strategy for achieving this. For example, once the EPA's Dallas office provided such training for state personnel in their region, they began working on individual improvement projects with each of their states. Their grant agreements then focused on commitment to improvement projects, rather than "beans" (number of inspections, reviews, and so on). As headquarters (HQ) employees visited states and the EPA regions, they participated in joint analyses of work processes and used some of the TQM analytical tools, such as flow charts, cause-and-effect diagrams, and pareto charts. In Louisiana, for example, the EPA-state team worked on a system to improve payment of claims for reimbursement from the state's tank trust fund. In New Mexico, they installed an expedited enforcement process, developed nationally but adopted and implemented locally.

This was a major change in the way the EPA managed and operated. OUST no longer believed that "we will do A and B will result." The organization invested completely in selling TQM as the way the EPA regions and headquarters and the states would do all their work. OUST management believed this would get much better results than other methods. Increasingly, OUST's state customers were demanding TQM training and beginning to expect TQM-type behavior from EPA headquarters and regional personnel. The regions, in turn, expected it from us in Washington. Sometimes this showed up in funny ways. For example, a fax was sent from headquarters to the regions requesting extra data from the states, which brought a return fax from the Kansas City office saying simply, "Is this value added?" This was enough to kill the request.

The role of management in TQM began to change, between organizations and within organizations. As the national program manager, the EPA headquarters stopped worrying about meeting numerical targets and started worrying about facilitating improved performance in the field. In traditional management systems, managers must develop the method by which work is accomplished. In a traditional labor-management relationship, these procedures may be the subject of contractual agreements on work rules. Under TQM, management shares responsibility for analyzing work processes with employees, although management must still decide on which work procedures should be used. It is management's responsibility to create a work environment where employee analysis of work is encouraged and rewarded. This facilitation role is not new for management, but the heavy emphasis on eliciting worker analysis and generating suggested improvements in work processes *is* new. A TQM organization spends much more of its time discussing, measuring, and analyzing how work gets done.

Ideology of Encouraging Improvement

Encouraging improvement, as opposed to meeting production targets, requires a paradigm shift for management theorists and practitioners. It is relatively easy to set an arbitrary numerical production quota without information. All management needs to do is pick a number higher than this year's total and "go for it." In fact, there is a sort of management machismo about how high you can go, or how "hard-nosed" and tough-minded a manager you can be. The tough-minded manager holds his or her workers "feet to the fire" and simply demands performance. Of course, performance is measured with surrogate measures of production or performance indicators, which may or may not be measuring what management thinks they are measuring.

TQM requires a more profound and substantial understanding of performance. Management must get real information in great detail about all aspects of production. Management indicators play a radically different role under TQM than in traditional management and are used to trigger more detailed analyses of production systems. They are also directed toward specific elements of the production process being targeted for improvement. For example, in measuring the number of environmentally safe tanks installed in a given state, we do not stop with the number of tanks installed; we look at the process of installing tanks and issuing permits for new tanks. If we are looking at the permit process, we do not stop with a count of the number of permits issued, or even the average time to issue a permit. We develop a flow chart and measure performance variation at each step. Our aim is to develop standard operating procedures for each element of the production process that reduces variation and errors made at each step.

Obviously, for this approach to be successful, management must facilitate an almost ruthless analysis of current levels of performance. They must constantly ask and train their employees to ask: What is really happening here? This requires an extreme degree of honesty in appraising performance. Often public agencies are afraid to evaluate programs because even a perception of failure can result in political problems. Fortunately, TQM work analysis is at a far more detailed level of analysis than traditional social science program evaluation. Typically, you are not attempting to assess the worth of an entire program but rather are focusing on a fairly specific element of a production process. Data on the amount of variation in the time it takes to review a draft position description are not likely to be front-page news in the *New York Times*.

These analyses are critical because you cannot rely on improvement as a way of increasing productivity if you do not know what your organization is producing and how production processes occur. Once work analysis is integrated into an organization's culture, it is possible to focus on improvement, but first management and employees must learn to define success. What type of changed performance constitutes an improvement?

The key to defining success is to ascertain the needs or wants of your customers. Analyzing public-sector customers is often a complex process, as you may have multiple customers whose needs conflict. It is not as simple as a private company that must "simply" define a market niche, see who wants the product, and refine the product to meet the customer's evolving needs. In the private sector, you assume that you can focus your analysis on a discrete, finite group of customers: if someone hates Big Macs they can always buy Whoppers. In government, agencies often have monopolies on particular products and services in a given geographic area—customers may be a more amorphous group. Nevertheless, although it is a more difficult task, public managers must still determine who their customers are and derive the definition of quality improvement from customer demands.

Improving the delivery of services to an agency's customers thus becomes more important under TQM than meeting numerical targets embedded in a rigid set of management indicators. Surrogate measures are abandoned and replaced by more detailed assessments of management performance. For managers, this means that goals are constantly evolving and being quantified in terms of customer satisfaction. Employees are directed to change organizational behavior to meet customer needs as they evolve rather than management needs that involve reaching some predetermined target. The organization attempts to continually get better at what it does rather than seek some abstract and arbitrary definition of success. Management's job is to engender this change in orientation.

Substituting Constant Improvement for Numerical Quotas

Some argue that without numerical targets, management becomes too "touchy feely" and organizational direction becomes too inexact, particularly in the public sector where management has no bottom-line profit-or-loss figure to measure success against. It is difficult, but important, to resist an almost natural tendency to manage through targets.

Avoiding Numerical Targets and Snappy Slogans

Nancy R. Mann, quoting from Brian Joiner and Peter Scholtes, observed that "when measurable controls or goals are unattainable or impractical, individuals and groups tend to fabricate conformance. . . . The greater the stress on reaching unattainable goals, especially when someone's career is on the line, the more likely it is that figures will be juggled" (Mann, 1985, p. 132). How often have you seen or been involved in situations where management says, "We have to do more. Let's increase all targets or quotas or goals for next year by 10 percent"? How do they expect this to happen? What is going to be changed from last year to bring about this 10 percent improvement? They do not know—they are just wishing it will happen. Too many managers believe that simply setting a tough performance standard will force the improvement to occur, including legislative bodies, budget bureaus, and public interest and lobbying groups in the public sector. Here is a place where we agree wholeheartedly with several of Deming's well-known fourteen points. According to Deming, management should "eliminate slogans, exhortations, and targets for the work force asking for zero defects and new levels of productivity. Such exhortations only create adversarial relationships, as the bulk of the causes of low quality and low productivity belong to the system and thus lie beyond the power of the work force. . . . Eliminate work standards (quotas) on the factory floor. Substitute leadership. . . . Eliminate management by objective. Eliminate management by numbers, numerical goals. Substitute leadership" (Deming, 1986, p. 24).

Another aspect of this approach is the use of slogans. For example, the EPA at one point gave out buttons that read "EPA QUALITY." People wore them, but their behavior did not change. Why? Because they did not know what they needed to do to bring about improved quality. We believe slogans are fine if they flow from work undertaken based on an assessment of where you are and where you want to be, which in turn is based on an understanding of the current process and its capability.

The story is frequently told about factory operations where the management sends a clear signal on what they think of quality. They tell the foreman to ship a flawed product to meet a customer's schedule—even though it will mean returned goods and rework later. We see the same thing in public-sector organizations all the time. For example, why is it that in program after program one-third of the work is completed in the first three-quarters of the year and two-thirds is pushed through in the last quarter? In fact, it frequently gets done in the last week or month of the last quarter. What does this say to the workers and midlevel managers? As one manager told us, "I've got to move those grants (or permits, enforcement actions, contracts) out the door by September 30. We take whatever shortcuts are necessary knowing that we are creating problems and work for future months and years." Can you see the similarity with the factory shipping flawed products?

Even when we get improved performance in quality or productivity in government, it is frequently labeled a failure. Why is this? It fails to meet a quota or target that someone set. Table 3.1 is taken from an actual situation in one agency. How was this performance viewed? Management all the way up the line considered this a failure. Although the workers had improved by 50 percent per year, their performance standards were tied to these targets. Worse yet, their performances were officially considered inadequate. The employees worried because the difference between getting an outstanding rating versus a satisfactory rating could affect future promotions, training opportunities, and pay. If it was a field or regional organization, it was marked as a failure at headquarters.

What did they fail to do? They failed to achieve a target set by someone else and frequently agreed to under duress. Did those who set the target know what the real work was? No. Did those who set the target suggest or know any ways to improve performance, other than pronouncements to work smarter or work harder? Did they use or provide training in TQM to the workers and managers so that they could identify and remove barriers to improved performance? Did they genuinely ask the workers what the problems were and then really listen? Of course they did not, because they too did not know how to work in this way.

The same thing applies in designing new programs or

Table 3.1. Sample Data for an Organization Managed by Targets.

Year	Units Completed	Target	Cumulative Shortfall
1988	14	17	−3
1989	21	25	−7
1990	32	36	−11

processes. OMB, Congress, or the agency head provides ten positions to set up a new process. No one knows exactly how the process is to be carried out or what its capacity will be in either quality or quantity at that time, yet they set a target of so many responses to emergencies or inspections or permits completed. More often the target is established informally by the number of items that the process is faced with handling in its first year. Then the manager is stuck with that target and judged by his or her success in meeting it. This results in situations where individuals face workloads of 100, 150, or 200 cases per worker. Do we expect quality work under such situations? Worse yet, what kind of signal is this sending to the workers about quality? How does it make them feel about their work and themselves?

We are convinced that Deming, Shigeo Shingo, and Taichi Ohno are absolutely right. *Targets are limiting.* The better way is to help workers learn to use work analysis tools so they can develop improvements and achieve levels of performance beyond what any manager would have the nerve to demand. Communicate TQM by focusing employees on improving the current level of performance rather than reaching artificial targets.

Can this really work? Here is an example from our personal experience in the OUST program. The EPA was unexpectedly appropriated funds for a new petroleum release fund to be used by states to clean up tank releases, where owners could not pay for the necessary corrective actions. This meant developing, negotiating, and completing cooperative agreements (a form of grant agreement) with state governments, a process that took one year and a great deal of paperwork in the existing system in the agency. When the agency received the appropriation, there were three months left in the fiscal year to negotiate the agreements and obligate the funds.

When pressed by the boss, the comptroller's office, and OMB, Brand refused to set a target and predict how many agreements would be completed. The truth was that no one knew, but the budget process and the planning and accountability system all demand that you set a target. OUST refused to do this. Brand considered setting a target. He consulted with his employees and asked, "What if I am forced to give a number, what do you think we might do?" After talking with the regional staff, the people who had to hammer out agreements with the states, they said they might hit fifteen completed agreements by September 30. But Brand never used the number, never set it as a target—even informally. The regions and the headquarters team just kept solving problems and achieved forty-four completed agreements by the deadline. Since no one had ever done this before, how could anyone set an intelligent target? If Brand had set the target at fifteen, the staff's best guess, OUST would never have reached forty-four.

This is why we disagree with those who advocate setting an improvement target when a team starts an improvement project. For example, in the Chicago office of the federal EPA, a team was organized to improve the processing and approval system for providing additional funding for cleaning up toxic waste dumps. When the EPA first created a flow chart and documented the current process, they found the average time was twenty-one days. They did not set a goal for how much they would improve but instead applied TQM methods to the process and kept making improvements. At the end of five months they had implemented changes that had lowered the average time to four days, a reduction of over 80 percent in processing time. Who would have dared set such a goal at the start of the project? What would its impact have been on the team? How would you come up with the number to set as the goal? Incidentally, the team continues to find ways to improve the quality and reduce the cost and the time needed to approve cleanup funding.

Numerical targets are frequently a substitute for human interaction, especially between management and labor. We have the illusion that setting an organizational target is like setting an individual target: if we did twenty-five pushups each day last week, certainly we can reach twenty-eight next week. Organizations are more complex than that. We may have reached twenty-five last week due to factors that cannot be duplicated this week.

One of the underlying problems with numerical targets is the games that organizations play in setting these targets. A dynamic is established where those who do the work attempt to underestimate what they might accomplish and those not responsible for the work, but higher in the hierarchy, attempt to set higher goals. Goal setting becomes a political process where the unit with the most control over the goal-setting process sets the goals. The workers attempt to utilize their control of information about current performance and the nature of real work to drive the goal down. Management attempts to drive the goals up through simple assertions of authority.

A final and perhaps more significant argument against targets is that they limit rather than promote accomplishment. If the workers find themselves faced with an unrealistic goal, for example, they adopt the traditional industrial method for meeting unrealistic quotas—perfected in its classic form in the former Soviet Union. The technique is known as "storming." When the deadline draws near, people work fast and furiously to manufacture and ship the goods, and quality becomes the lowest priority. We have a rather natural tendency to relax when the target is within reach, when we might easily have exceeded the target if there were, in fact, no target at all.

Advantage of Improvement as a Goal

The chief advantage of improvement as a goal is that it forces management to understand the organization's real work and its current level of performance. It also requires management to understand the capacity of their systems: what their organizations are capable of producing. Goals cannot be set in a vacuum and must be derived from such a meaningful understanding of the organization's work, grounding management in the reality of the shop floor (or its functional equivalent in public-sector service organizations).

A focus on improvement allows for small victories early in the process; employees achieve goals that they can "see"; management rewards small improvements, or a simple reversal in negative trends. (This can be very important in a troubled organization in need of a turnaround.) Finally, the emphasis on improvement can help prevent declining performance, which often occurs when an organization focuses on a big victory and neglects or risks its "base" to accomplish that type of win.

Reliance on Worker Analysis

Here is a familiar scene in many organizations: highly competent professionals receive grant applications, review them, ask for additional information from grantees, consider a number of criteria and variables, and write recommendations for funding approved grants. They know how to do analysis, but when they want to devote time to assessing the way they do this work and to improving it, management tells them to forget it. "We don't have time for that," they say; or else, "They won't let us make any changes in the process." So both workers and managers continue to struggle with an ever-increasing backlog of work, loads of rework, and deteriorating service to their clientele.

Focusing Employee Analysts on Their Own Tasks

Management work is often seen as the development of work procedures and strategies that will interact effectively with the organization's environment. Although the selection of an organization's overall direction and customers remains the work of management, TQM seeks to involve employees in the analysis of their own tasks. In government, the workers rarely focus their analytical talent on their own work: TQM not only permits such analysis but requires it. This reliance is a major change in traditional management practice. It unleashes an untapped source of analytical talent in your employees and enables it to be directed toward the way your organization does its work. It also changes the power relationship between employees and management because if TQM is to work, each has a unique contribution to make.

Advantages of Modifying the Power Relationship Between Employees and Management

Under TQM, management shares responsibility with workers for establishing and improving work process systems. This concept changes one of the traditional roles of management: its dominance on thinking about operations. It must also share decision-making authority (though not final responsibility) over work processes. This may make management of operations more time-consuming and complex but often more effective, because employees provide more accurate information about operations (since they are the people who actually perform the tasks).

A New Paradigm for Defining Excellence in Public Management

The definition of the effective public manager changes under TQM. The old model is detailed in Cohen's *The Effective Public Manager* (1988). This is the manager who can work around the rules and get the job done—the bureaucrat. Under the new paradigm, the effective public manager does not accept the rules as given.

The Old Paradigm: The Bureaucrat

At a recent meeting of the Association for Public Policy Analysis and Management, Michael Barzalay of Harvard University noted that one of the more important features of TQM is that it provides a new paradigm for assessing management excellence. We agree, and we believe that this reconceptualization of excellence is one of the most significant changes that TQM may bring to government.

Public-sector practitioners are familiar with the image of the consummate bureaucrat—the individual who knows the rules, can get the job done within the system, and stays out of trouble. This manager is not concerned about customers and quality and is not really concerned about policy. The bureaucrat is the pure administrator, the person who can take direction from a political leader and move paper to the right places to make sure that the money is spent, the contracts are let, the people are hired, and the desired output is produced. Many of us who have spent a good deal of time in government can conjure up images of specific people who fit this description.

What is key here is that these people do not question the rules or attempt to improve standard operating procedures (SOPs); they are just very good at manipulating those procedures to force certain desired outcomes. They make "things" happen and they get "things" done. They do not take the time to consider whether what they accomplish is worth doing.

The New Paradigm: The Effective Total Quality Manager

Under TQM, the consummate bureaucrat is a well-intentioned anachronism. The customer and quality are the paramount values; the system is no longer sacrosanct. Understanding the rules and working within them are less important—adapting the rules and changing work processes to achieve quality are more valued. Understanding current rules and procedures is valued only as a means of understanding the current level of performance, a necessary but no longer sufficient condition of excellence in management.

Under the new paradigm, a manager frequently asks questions about work processes: Is this step needed? Can this step be improved? Who is the customer of this work? Of course such questions must be followed by actions. New procedures must be tried and evaluated; work does not halt while we sit back and think about it. Often processes that we suspect are less than useful are continued until a better substitute is developed; however, a great value is placed on the creative manager who can question current practice and stimulate employees to develop new, more productive work procedures.

TQM forces excellent public managers to go beyond learning to manipulate the complex processes of government and to gauge the effect of the organization's programs on real customers. Getting a contract out remains critical, but it is no longer an end in itself. Under the new paradigm, an effective manager might question the contract itself, kill the request for proposal (RFP), and get the work done in some simpler, quicker, and less expensive way. Or this manager might decide that work being done by the contract is not needed at all or is in need of radical modification.

Is This Really a Revolution?

We have seen a number of other so-called "management revolutions" come and go, and so we are reluctant to predict the long-term impact of this one.

A number of other management innovations, ranging from management by objectives (MBO) to organizational development (OD), focused our attention on getting better performance from groups and individuals as part of organizations. Management scholars and practitioners have long been concerned with stimulating complex organizations to accomplish goals, while developing and maintaining organizational capability and morale. We do not argue that the ideas in TQM are particularly new or revolutionary.

In many respects, TQM represents a synthesis of a variety of trends in the world of management: (1) renewed emphasis on the production line as a focus of management attention; (2) the use of increasingly sophisticated statistical techniques to help understand production processes; (3) reduction in levels of hierarchy in organizations; (4) increased use of production workers in analysis of work; (5) greater worker involvement with management in decision making; and (6) increased use of groups and teams to solve problems.

Many of TQM's component elements have existed for some time. We do find that the major emphasis on starting with the customer's needs (being customer-driven) is a unique aspect of TQM. However, what is new and different about TQM is the synthesis of these elements into a single conceptual framework.

What we find revolutionary is the combination of "hard" management techniques, such as statistical process control and managing with detailed data on operations, with "soft" management techniques, such as learning to work in groups, amnesty, "drive out fear," and involving everyone in the analysis of work processes. We know that managers must focus on specific performance indicators to understand what the organization is doing. However, under TQM, you do not simply grade employee performance from above: you work together to collect meaningful information about performance—in fact, to decide what information is meaningful; you work together to develop ways to improve performance.

We want to be careful not to overstate what TQM is and what it can help deliver. In some ways it is really an academic rather than practical issue to try to determine whether TQM is something new under the sun. Our experience has been that these ideas are useful to managers and can help organizations work better.

For the people or organizations who decide to learn all they can about this way of working, who work at understanding the theory and Deming's principles, who struggle to make TQM pervade every aspect of their work, and who persist over months and years, significant improvements and breakthroughs can be and have been achieved.

PART TWO

Implementing
Total Quality Management
in
Public Organizations

CHAPTER 4

Getting Prepared:
Understanding and Overcoming
Barriers to Change

This chapter discusses why people and organizations resist change. In many ways it is different from the other chapters in the book, as it steps back from the practice of TQM and discusses some of the basic themes of organizational theory. TQM involves fundamental changes in how organizations operate. If you are to succeed at bringing TQM into your organization, we think it is important that you understand these general factors that influence organizational behavior. This knowledge will help you understand and overcome the obstacles to implementing TQM in your own organization. Each organization has its own unique environment, goals, social structure, and culture. At many times in this book, we will say, "You must adapt the techniques of TQM to your own organizational setting." This chapter is designed to provide you with a framework for a deeper understanding of that organizational setting.

Bureaucracy and Stability

One of the major questions we often face when discussing TQM with those who have attempted to utilize it is: Why is TQM so hard to bring into an organization? Why do people resist it and why is it so hard for organizations to stick to this new way of working? Adjusting work processes to new conditions and improving them so they work better seems like the common sense thing to do, but organizations can find constant modifications of standard operating procedures unsettling and disruptive.

Why do organizations resist change? Part of the answer lies in fundamental features of the bureaucratic form of organization. Bureaucracy is designed to allow large groups of people to break down complex tasks into simple component elements. Work that is broken down into its constituent parts is said to be differentiated, a segmentation that then creates the need to bring the separate pieces back together, a function known as coordination. Organizations are complex interconnected organisms, held together and made productive by a set of formal and informal relationships that evolve gradually, over time. The networks of relationships and interaction are persistent and often continue past the point at which they are functional, often persisting after changes in the organization's environment or mission make them irrelevant or unnecessary.

As organizational theorists such as Chester Barnard and Philip Selznick understood, the SOPs and relationships in an organization eventually become valued by its members for what they are rather than for what they do. People get comfortable with the organization's way of operating, feel secure in their tasks and sense of belonging, and resist anything that disrupts the cozy arrangement. Since the workers in the organization know their highly specialized or differentiated work better than anyone else, efforts by outside coordinators, managers, or analysts to understand and change their work are likely to be resisted.

This is why TQM's emphasis on worker self-analysis or a worker's analysis of his or her own work process is so critical. An organization can only change as much as its members are willing to change. When workers analyze a work process, they can factor into their analysis their own ability to change the way they perform their own tasks. The very term "standard operating procedure" provides an indication of the value that bureaucracy places on stability: the effort is to operate according to procedures that are standard—always the same. TQM requires that SOPs be seen as uniform and predictable but also as constantly evolving operating procedures, which is a major change in the way that bureaucratic organizations operate. The traditional satisficing criterion (March and Simon, 1958) that a "good" SOP is one that works acceptably well no longer holds. Under TQM, SOPs must constantly be improved to respond to the escalating expectations and competitive demands of a rapidly changing society and economy.

It is not yet clear that the traditional bureaucratic form can be adapted to TQM's requirement of constant change. It seems clear to us that the contemporary environment of public organizations requires organizations to develop their ability to adapt and rapidly change. To discuss the concept of change in public-sector organizations, it is necessary to examine the nature of the environments in which they operate, their cultures, and their structures and standard processes. The remainder of this chapter examines these fundamental concepts of organization theory, which practitioners must be aware of and understand if they hope to serve as organizational change agents. This analysis of organizational fundamentals can identify potential impediments to TQM implementation, as well as factors that may encourage organizational change. You will then have a better idea of what you are up against and how to approach problems that may develop when you initiate change efforts.

The Organization's Environment

According to systems theory, organizations can be thought of as open systems that interact in various ways with their external environments (Beer, 1980). Many similarities exist in the ways in which public- and private-sector organizations interact with their respective external environments, but there are, however, many important differences. Public-sector organizations typically operate in fluid, highly politicized environments—intensely scrutinized by the media, forced to adhere to a number of rigid les and constraints, and often subjected to the changing views and needs of elected officials. Given these significant environmental differences, it is clear that public-sector organizations face unique challenges when attempting to implement organizational changes such as TQM.

No organization is free to set whatever goals it wishes to set. Similarly, no organization is ever free to appeal to whatever customer they wish to appeal to. However, public organizations are often more highly constrained in selecting goals and customers. These choices are often made in advance by elected officials. These environmental factors do not prevent the use of TQM as a method of working, but they affect the type of quality improvements that are feasible in public organizations. For example, a public manager may decide that a certain administrative process is redundant or silly but may be required by law to complete the process.

The four primary aspects of the public-sector organizational environment are (1) the political environment, (2) the economic environment, (3) the social environment, and (4) the technological environment. The political environment is made up of the legislative branch, the remainder of the executive branch, the judicial branch, interest groups, and the political views of the broad public and various politically active elites. The economic environment is defined and influenced by the organization's program, its role in the private economic market, and the economy's relative health. The social environment includes those values and norms held by the society that directly affect the organization's functions and programs. The technological environment is characterized by the rate at which the technology used or produced by the organization changes. The various political, economic, social, and technological environments unique to public-sector organizations each have characteristics that can impede or facilitate change.

Political Environment

Public-sector organizations are, by nature, political entities that are easily disrupted by power struggles. Conflict often occurs between agency personnel, committed to the organization's stated mission, and politicians, who, for one reason or another, find it politically expedient to undercut the organization, sometimes making it quite difficult for it to function effectively or efficiently. Often, conflict between legislators and the elected chief executive can place an agency uncomfortably in the middle.

In some cases, the organization's expertise leads it to oppose the formal boss at the top of the executive branch. At other times the organization finds itself wanting to oppose the views of powerful legislators or interest groups. When the political environment is particularly volatile, "laying low" is the preferred strategy of the seasoned bureaucrat. Since change, in and of itself, is frequently considered risky and likely to attract unwanted attention from political players, public managers usually prefer a more low-key conservative or bureaucratic style to minimize political interference in the organization's operations. Under these conditions, it can be difficult to convince agency leadership and staff that a new work strategy like TQM is worth the risk. On the other hand, the day-to-day practice of politics places demands for results on organizations that can help change agents in a bureaucracy to prevail.

Economic Environment

Within the economic environment, public-sector organizations face other problems. An unhealthy economy can lead to uncertain funding. State and local governments, not allowed to print their own money and run at a deficit, are particularly vulnerable to rapid changes in tax revenues. As jurisdictions have attempted to diversify their revenue sources, even sophisticated budget shops have a difficult time predicting expected revenues. This creates an atmosphere of helplessness or fear of change that inhibits change efforts.

On the other hand, fiscal pressures are often cited as an important potential catalyst for change in public-sector organizations. When an agency experiences budget cuts and hiring freezes, managers are forced to try to accomplish just as much, or more, with fewer resources. Cutbacks can have two effects: they can impede change by encouraging an "us against them" attitude, or they can cause managers to think critically about the systems and strategies they use. Often this self-examination facilitates the process of organizational redesign. Staff sometimes have to be shown that the strict rules governing things like codes of conduct and procurement procedures can be overcome so that an organization can achieve innovation, creative thinking, and organizational change.

Social Environment

An organization's social environment is the sphere of interaction between the organization and the community at large. Most agencies have a great deal of influence with the groups of people in society that directly benefit, or suffer, from the agency's policies and activities. The rapport that an agency has with its interest groups, clients, or customers is extremely important. If people feel that an agency contributes to their safety or well-being, the agency may have an easier time performing its appointed functions. In addition, the agency's work may receive support or opposition from the broader society, including groups that are not directly affected by the organization. Social acceptance and enthusiasm for an organization's work can lead to voluntary assistance, public cooperation, and a fertile environment for developing political (and budget) support. Social opposition, on the other hand, can impair an organization's well-being.

Hostile and supportive social environments will not translate automatically into hostility against or support for organizational change. In some cases, a supportive social environment will give an organization's leaders greater leeway and flexibility to create change. In other cases, it may lead the organization to be fat, happy, and wasteful, knowing that whatever it does, it will continue to enjoy popular support and resources. When the environment is tougher, it may cause bureaucrats to hunker down and resist change, or conversely, it may convince them that radical steps are needed to build social acceptance and popular support.

In any event, managers seeking to be change agents must be aware of the organization's social environment. They must attempt to understand the effect of that environment on the perceptions and values of the agency's management and staff.

Technological Environment

An organization's technological environment is characterized by the technologies used or produced by the agency. Technological change tends to facilitate rather than impede organizational change. New technologies can trigger fundamental organizational change in two ways: first, they can change the way people work; second, they can affect the organization's mission. Office technologies such as word processing, personal computers, and voice mail have changed the role of clerical and professional staff and influenced the way organizations conduct their work. Clerical staff may not type as much as they used to, but the sheer volume of information processed by many offices has made clerical staff, in many organizations, information coordinators.

Changing technologies can affect an organization's mission by changing the conditions and problems that it must address. Environmental pollution is, of course, the best example of a policy problem that changes as production technologies change, but many other examples of technology influence an agency's mission. Certainly police work has changed as automatic weapons become lighter and more common, satellite communication has changed the nature of telecommunications regulation, and expectations of adequate health care have changed with the development of modern medical technology.

Importance of the Organization's Environment

The various dimensions of an organization's external environment shape the work process by providing, or failing to provide, the resources necessary to accomplish specific objectives. Thus, all organizations are subject to environmental influences. In fact, some theorists have suggested that the manager's accessibility to important environmental information is perhaps the most important variable in determining the structure of an organization (Lawrence and Lorsch, 1967b). According to this model, the gap between the information that the manager *has* and the information that the manager *needs* represents uncertainty. The size of the gap can determine whether or not an organization consistently achieves its objectives. Thus, a critical assessment of an organization's environment is necessary when considering organizational change, since the fluidity, or rigidity, of the environment can have a significant impact on efforts toward change.

The organizations that build change and adaptation into their standard operating procedures are the ones that best respond to a rapidly changing external environment. This requires the development of an organizational culture that is constantly adapting itself to the environment in which it operates. For this culture to develop within an organization, every employee must be convinced that change is *normal* and not something to be afraid of. The next section discusses the relationship between organizational culture and organizational change.

Organizational Culture

Organizational culture is another important concept to consider when assessing an organization's capacity for adapting itself to TQM. The culture of an organization can be thought of as a shared set of informal beliefs and values that make up the ground rules for what is expected from employees and what employees can expect from an organization. An organization's culture is analogous to an individual's personality, or self-concept. It is a shared ideology, a collective consciousness, that organizes and guides behavior patterns. Organizational culture is a somewhat slippery concept, given its phenomenological nature, and has often been overlooked, or simply ignored, by researchers interested in organizational change and work behavior (Beer, 1980). More recently, however, organizational development professionals have begun to recognize that organizational culture is an extremely influential force that both motivates and discourages certain kinds of individual or group behavior within organizations.

Function and Nature of Public Organizational Culture

Organizational culture serves as a binding mechanism in the sense that the strength of the culture is positively related to the degree to which an actual number of beliefs and values are held in common by the employees. The more people in an organization who share beliefs, the more influence the culture will have on individual behavior within the organization. A strong sense of organizational culture can thus be a positive thing, both resulting from and creating a shared sense of vision and purpose among employees.

Organizational culture in public-sector organizations is typically based on a set of primary values, or according to Gerald Caiden, an "ideology of public service." Characteristics of this ideology can be summarized as follows:

1. Government is an instrument for carrying out the will of the people, as defined by their elected representatives.
2. Public officials are elected, appointed, or hired to serve the interests of the public.
3. Public officials should avoid even the appearance of impropriety and always maintain the highest ethical standards.
4. Civil servants should always be mindful of economic and efficiency concerns.
5. Public officials have a duty to obey their superiors and put their personal interests and concerns aside. If a public official has personal objections to a particular policy, he or she should leave public office before publicly voicing any opposition to that policy.
6. Public officials should be appointed to office based on merit and their degree of fitness for the office in question.
7. Public-sector employees should be held to the same legal standards as everyone else (Caiden, 1981).

The values above represent generalizations about the cultures in various public agencies. There are, of course, variations in the degree of emphasis that any agency may place on these values, depending on its mission. These differences ultimately mean that some agencies have more latitude than others in observing these rules, depending in part on the external environment in which the agency operates. There are also mission-specific or mission-related organizational culture traits: at the EPA a high value is placed on adherence to scientific data; in police departments, defense of colleagues is often firmly entrenched in organizational culture.

Organizational Culture and Organizational Change

Cultural norms have a significant impact on an organization's ability to change. Many behavior patterns are held in common by most types of organizations and are deeply ingrained—for example, do not ever disagree with the boss; do not give the boss any bad news; do not share information with co-workers. These are almost instinctive and can act as real barriers to change in any organization, even in organizations that have begun quality improvement efforts. People in work groups, for example, can unwittingly encourage each other to continue in negative behavior patterns such as those noted above. The average worker does not want to be the one to tell the supervisor: you are the reason that things never get done on time. In general, organizations and people resist change when they have some type of investment in particular work patterns or organizational arrangements, and this resistance is likely to increase at a rate proportional to that investment.

It is important to note that, especially in large organizations, there can be more than one set of belief systems and cultural differences in organization units by function or mission, or between hierarchical levels. In this way, we can think of different groups within organizations as social learning systems. The interactions between and within these circles can serve to socialize new members and keep everyone's behavior within certain established limits.

Psychologists and learning theorists have long recognized the importance of concepts like reinforcement and modeling on learned human behavior patterns. Reinforcement in organizations involves things like promotions, salary increases, recognition, general job satisfaction, responsibility, authority, and even office space or furniture. These are not always easy for public-sector managers to provide; the strict nature of civil service rules can limit the use of such tools as reinforcement or incentives. Part of your strategy in implementing TQM may involve more informal reward systems, such as public recognition or personal thanks. We tend to underestimate the positive effect of people seeing their ideas put in place with the resulting visible improvements and reduction in frustration and the redoing of work. John J. Hudiberg of Florida Power and Light tells how "our employees told us that the most meaningful form of recognition was seeing their ideas implemented and producing results. Next in importance was having their supervisors and fellow workers know who did it and appreciate their accomplishments" (Hudiburg, 1991, p. 116). Limits on a manager's ability to reward, punish, or fire within the scope of the rules can make it difficult to change deeply ingrained behavior patterns. Employees can be particularly reluctant to accept the idea that they do not have to be afraid to tell the truth. Reinforcement by managers, in the form of some type of reward (perhaps even a simple thank-you) can go a long way. Established socialization mechanisms can reinforce negative behaviors in an organization's culture and thus impede change. For example, Brand encountered some barriers when he tried to meet with and hear directly from one of his key customers and suppliers: the Underground Tank state program directors. The regional offices had a long-standing practice that all contacts with state directors should be through them. This was not merely whim on their part, as they had suffered through various blunders by headquarters in the past.

People in organizations also learn through social modeling—imitating the behavior of other people in the organization who are successful or hold high status. This concept can work to a manager's advantage when attempting to change behavior. If people see the manager behaving a certain way, with successful outcomes, they are more likely to imitate that behavior. Given this concept, it is easy to see how your own support for and active participation in TQM efforts can make a tremendous difference.

Implementing TQM will require a direct effort to reeducate your staff to adopt a new culture. If, in trying to implement change, you fail to address the issue of established organizational culture, all your best efforts may be thwarted by behaviors that people do not necessarily know they are perpetuating. For this reason, you must work toward changing the socialization mechanisms in your organization. Incentive systems, leadership by example, increased communication, and the development of new group norms are all strategies that can change the psychology, and therefore the culture, of your organization.

In doing so, however, you may encounter resistance from other managers, who will be required to examine their own value systems. Change is often the most frightening to people who fear that they have the most to lose. Therefore, it is extremely important that managers and change agents attempt to "visualize culture and verbalize it" (Beer, 1980, p. 36). In this way, you gain an important understanding of the subtle behavior patterns in your organization and how its culture will affect efforts to implement TQM. For TQM to succeed, it is absolutely essential that top managers learn to accept the importance of flexibility and innovation.

Organizational Structure and Standard Processes

It is difficult to think about an organization's culture without thinking about its structure as well. The terms *organizational structure* and *standard processes* refer to the more formal, coordinating aspects. These include job descriptions, standard operating procedures, formal meetings, personnel policies and systems, hierarchical relationships, labor relations policies, accounting and budgeting systems, and even physical layout. In order to understand how your organization's structure might help or hinder your efforts to begin TQM, it is useful to explore the concepts of organizational structure and standard processes.

Structures and standard processes are used by management in all organizations for the purpose of obtaining desired behavior. Incentives such as pay scales, rewards, and career ladders are all designed to obtain high degrees of effort from people. Organizational structure also acts to shape the psychological environment of an organization, since employee behavior and attitudes are significantly influenced by the context within which they work. We are primarily interested in those characteristics of structure and process that most relate to public bureaucracies.

Perhaps one of the most obvious characteristics of public bureaucracies is the degree to which specific jobs and procedures are standardized and organized into formal units. As Max Weber (1946) noted, formal hierarchy is a defining characteristic of bureaucracy. Everyone in an organization must have a clear understanding of whom they are working for or with and who is working for them. As noted at the start of this chapter, bureaucracy has, as its greatest strength, the ability to break up work into small, efficiently performed tasks, each performed by a distinct organizational unit. This division of labor allows organizational units to develop great expertise and facility with specific, narrowly defined tasks. Bureaucracies assume they operate in fairly stable external environments and devote a great deal of effort to acting in a rational way (Mintzberg, 1973a).

Efficiency is the primary objective in bureaucratic operations (Mintzberg, 1973a), and efforts toward efficiency have traditionally centered on SOPs. Standard operating procedures, as we have discussed before, allow organizations to create specific, by-the-book rules about work processes in an effort to eliminate variation in tasks that are performed over and over again by different people. They are used almost universally in public-sector organizations.

Some earlier writings on organizational structure suggest that standardized procedures, formal rules systems, and highly compartmentalized job responsibilities can have negative impacts on human behavior patterns and on efforts to undertake change in an organization. Merton (1940) suggests that the rigid rules and systems inherent in a bureaucracy act as cues to inform employees about the lowest level of performance that is acceptable. In other words, setting minimum standards will encourage employees to do only the absolute minimum of work required under the system. Their contribution to the organization will thus be minimized, and a culture of bureaucratic inertia may begin to develop. Managers often respond to this type of situation by trying to exert even more control by means of still more formal rules and procedures (Merton, 1940) or increased specialization (Selznick, 1949): the very devices that reduce flexibility and discourage innovation.

As we have seen, setting production quotas is a practice that is strongly discouraged under TQM. Quotas can have the effect of discouraging (or at least, *not* encouraging) performance levels above and beyond the bare minimum. Yet quota setting and other types of efficiency efforts (for example, increased specialization, more formalized rules) are integral parts of most bureaucratic structures and contribute to organizational rigidity.

Bureaucratic Structure, Standard Processes, and Organizational Change

It is important for managers to be aware of the impact of organizational structure and SOPs when attempting to encourage TQM-type behaviors in staff members. TQM demands innovation and creativity and thus conflicts with the thrust toward stability that is inherent in the bureaucratic form. Often people are reluctant to abandon stability for change, since stability is comfortable and reassuring. As a manager, you must find ways to reward innovation and ideas about how to neutralize, when possible, organizational rigidity. Standard operating procedures are certainly central to organizational functioning, but staff should be encouraged to think about them critically. If you educate your staff so that they are encouraged to think about the work processes they are performing, instead of blindly following SOPs, you may unleash all sorts of creative energy. Employees who are encouraged to be creative will often surprise you and will feel better about coming to work, especially when they feel that they have something important to contribute.

Understanding Resistance to Change

Although the factors discussed previously indicate that organizations will vary in their receptivity to change, overall they tend to resist change. To understand why this is true, it is important to take several factors into account. Rino Patti (1974) has identified four important variables in assessing organizational resistance: (1) the nature and type of the proposed change, (2) the style and value orientation of the decision maker, (3) the administrative distance between the decision maker and the person who proposes the change, and (4) "sunk costs," or the investments, financial or psychological, that the organization and/or managers have made in the system that the change agent intends to alter.

As Patti notes, there are two things to keep in mind when assessing the nature and type of any proposed change: the first is its possible scope or how many people or organizational units will be affected by it; the second is its depth. Change can be simply procedural, affecting the rules that guide daily work. At a medium level of depth, change can be programmatic, meaning that it is designed to modify operations so the organization can more effectively carry out its appointed mission. At its greatest depth, change can be basic, meaning that the change effort focuses on the agency's core set of objectives. Change efforts involving TQM will involve change at each of the three levels. Obviously, broad change proposals that encompass many different aspects of an organization will encounter the most resistance since the perceived (or actual) costs of change will be higher. This is one reason why, when choosing TQM projects, it is best to begin with small projects that other managers and superiors can support and also feel that they have little or nothing to lose by lending that support.

The second key factor when assessing resistance to change is the value system and decision-making style of your organizational superiors. Decision makers are considerably different in their responsiveness to proposed changes. Usually, a manager will make choices for the organization that are most likely to aid in achieving the goals that he or she feels are most important. Managers in the public sector probably have less leeway in this respect, since public-sector organizations are more regulated and constrained in both policy and practice. It is usually true, however, that managers have some room to maneuver and set priorities. If you are in a position to set your unit's priorities, you can direct your staff to work in a TQM way. If, on the other hand, you are a manager or staff person with less influence, you can still change your own work behaviors or approach supervisors with new ideas. Worker self-analysis is, after all, a vital component in successful TQM efforts. It is important, however, to keep management's perspective in mind when pushing for TQM or any organizational change. Meeting the concerns of managers above you is essential where their approval is necessary. For example, we have found that management is not usually interested in innovation, but can be sold on a change if they are shown that it lessens problems or the likelihood of problems. We have found that, whatever the bosses' proclaimed desires, what they really want is the absence of problems.

A third issue involves organizational distance, or the number of administrative levels between the person who is proposing the change and the person who ultimately has to approve it. Typically, the more levels through which a proposal must pass, the greater the chance for disagreement, misunderstanding, or conflict. As a proposal is "touched" by more and more people, its strength can be diluted, its purpose distorted by the value systems of intermediaries, or its timetable disrupted. Also, proposals that have to pass through several administrative levels are likely to conflict with proposals from other groups with competing interests.

If the superiors in your organization are TQM devotees, you are less likely to encounter such resistance, or if you do, it may be in a more enlightened form. If, on the other hand, most people in your organization are unfamiliar with TQM, you may encounter more resistance. Again, we cannot overemphasize the importance of beginning *small* improvement projects that are less likely to need clearance from above and will probably not require approvals. Laying low until you have successes to report may be a good strategy.

The fourth variable to keep in mind when assessing resistance to change involves sunk costs—the investments that have been made by people in an organization, or by the organization itself, that have developed, or served to perpetuate, certain behavior patterns and systems within the organization. These investments can be in the form of money, staff time, egos, personal commitment or satisfaction, or energy. This is a concept closely tied to the idea of organizational culture, since these are some of the elements that define and shape culture.

We sometimes think of bureaucracies as having almost a gravitational pull. Bureaucratic activity might be seen as an almost relentless tendency to resist change. Organizational change can be seen as a balloon that floats in the sky, until the gravitational force of bureaucratic structure and process brings it down to earth. This chapter has sought to identify the organizational characteristics that TQM change agents must understand and develop strategies to overcome. The next few chapters of the book provide guidance on how to implement TQM and overcome typical barriers to organizational change.

CHAPTER 5

Taking the First Steps:
Analyzing Your Work

Accepting the notion that we should analyze our own tasks is easy; doing it is hard. This chapter is designed to be an introduction to the analysis of work. We begin by discussing how you might organize for work analysis, when and how to establish, manage, and monitor a quality improvement team. We then discuss how to use the customer and supplier analysis we described in Chapter Three to improve work processes. Next, we discuss how to describe and analyze the work you do on your own or as part of a group. We also discuss the questions you must ask in conducting a work analysis and then detail a number of tools you can use to help answer those questions. The chapter concludes by presenting a case study of a specific work problem addressed through the use of work analysis.

Organizing for Work Analysis

Working in a TQM way *does not* require that every problem of improvement be tackled by a formally established team. An individual or a group conducting its regular work can utilize a TQM approach; that is, they can use TQM tools and talk with their customers and suppliers to anticipate and solve problems. With that important caveat, let us turn to team set-up.

When to Establish Quality Improvement Teams

One judgment you will need to make is the level of formality you give to the process of establishing TQM in your organization. As we have noted earlier, eventually you want all work to be TQM work, replacing the separateness and formality of your initial foray into TQM with a more informal, everyday approach. The best way to begin, in most organizations, is to identify a number of specific work areas and begin intensive quality improvement projects.

If you decide to transform your agency and integrate TQM into your organization's culture, a first step is to provide your staff with TQM orientation training, giving them background on TQM's core concepts and analytical methods. However, you should not confuse this training (which can be purchased from a wide variety of vendors) with full implementation of TQM. Training can help get you started, but TQM truly begins in an organization when teams are established to start analyzing and improving specific work processes. As Crosby (1984, p. 97) observes, "Concepts are essential, and the education to understand them is a must; however, nothing happens unless somebody actively does something. 'Doing something' in the case of quality improvement requires that actions be taken to actually change the culture and management style of the company."

When establishing your organization's first improvement teams, it is important to tackle problems that people in the organization consider important (Scholtes and others, 1988). However, it is also important to select a variety of types of problems; you want to ensure that your staff gets the message that TQM is a new way of working and is applicable to all types of work. Some improvement projects can address clerical problems such as inadequate filing and personal computer (PC) utilization; others can be programmatic, such as methods of delivering a specific service to a particular client group. It is important that some of the projects you select hold the potential for quick, visible, and measurable victories. Once you get the ball rolling, improvement projects should become part of the regular work of your organization. When a new responsibility is given to the office, and SOPs are established to carry out that responsibility, those procedures should be established with as clear an understanding of real work processes as possible. This includes using the principles of TQM in the design of the procedures. Have you determined who your suppliers are and what you need from them? Have you talked with them about the proposed procedures or included them on the design team? What about your customers? Have you talked only among yourselves because you believe that you know what the customer needs and wants? Or have you worked with customers to design the process?

At the EPA, for example, after a draft financial reporting procedure was developed, OUST was very concerned about the burden that it would place on its customers, the state underground tank regulating programs. The people involved worked hard to determine why every one of seventeen pieces of information was being required by the finance office, what it would take to obtain and report the information, and how it would be used (if at all). Over a two-month period, the project team reduced the reporting requirement to three pieces of information, by working in concert with their suppliers of financial data (the state program and budget offices) and the customer of their financial data (the federal finance office). By the time they agreed, everyone understood what was needed and why, which made for improved compliance once the procedure was put in place. When any problems came up, the team that had created the procedure handled them in accordance with TQM principles. Thus, there was no need for any kind of formal quality team—TQM was integrated into the regular work process.

How to Establish the Team

The method you use to establish a quality improvement team will vary depending on your organization's cultural characteristics and the stage you have reached in integrating TQM into your work processes (Crosby, 1984). You will know you have been successful when all new tasks assigned to your staff are designed by utilizing TQM work analysis.

The first phase of any project will be to analyze the existing level of performance, discuss and describe the production process, identify and work with suppliers, and identify and listen to your customers. Continuously focusing on these factors, and analyzing and improving work processes, must eventually become the approach to all of an organization's work.

However, in the process of establishing TQM in your organization, you need some explicit quality improvement teams and projects in order to demonstrate your commitment to this new way of working and to allow your staff to learn the rudiments of work analysis by actually practicing it. Exhibit 5.1 is a checklist that can be used in beginning an improvement project. It focuses the project team on the steps involved in analyzing a work process, and it helps identify data needs and focus improvement projects on specific, operational tasks.

The methods you use to select your first improvement teams, their composition, and their powers are critical decisions on the road to organizational transformation. You must address the following issues: How do I select teams? Whom do I put on these teams? What authority do the quality improvement teams have to make changes in work processes? How do these initial TQM projects relate to the organization's management structure?

Team Selection and Composition

After your staff receives some initial TQM training, you are then ready to establish your first quality improvement teams. When forming them, it is critical that they be made up of people who actually do the work being analyzed. If the work involves extensive interaction with other offices (such as contracts or budget offices), you will need to include people from those offices or people who understand how they work. Although you do not need to include everyone in your organization involved in the task, you should make certain that your team includes staff from as many levels of the hierarchy as feasible.

Exhibit 5.1. Quality Improvement Project Checklist.

1. What activity is the project seeking to improve?
2. Who is the project's team leader and who are the team's members?
3. What specific work process are you trying to improve?
4. How is this work process now performed?
5. What is the current level of performance of this work process?
6. Have you measured this level of performance? How?
7. What additional information or data do you need to measure the current level of performance more precisely?
8. How do you plan to collect or obtain this information?
9. What will you do with this information to analyze it once you have collected it?
10. What are the most significant obstacles to improving this work process?
11. Identify one (or possibly two) of these significant obstacles and develop a method for overcoming it.
12. Develop a pilot project to try out the work process improvement. What changes in procedure are you planning to institute?
    • How is the activity now done?
    • How will the activity change?
    Who will manage and staff the pilot project?
    How long will the project last?
    What is the definition of success?
    Who decides whether to institute this change throughout the organization?
13. To what degree has the pilot project improved the level of performance?
    What are the workhours, days, or months saved?
    Are you meeting customers' needs through improved quality?
    Have there been reductions in cost to your agency or your customers?
    Are you providing quicker service or increased productivity?
    Has there been a reduction in redoing work through the elimination of errors?
    What other measures have you taken?

These initial improvement teams are designed to achieve practical improvements in your organization's work and to be change agents within your organization. They should be set up to demonstrate the feasibility and usefulness of TQM work analysis and to train your staff on the day-to-day operational techniques of work analysis. Your purpose in selecting members for these first teams is partly political: you are attempting to convince a usually skeptical staff that you are committed to TQM and that it can work. When selecting leaders for the improvement teams, do not limit yourself to your current managers—appoint staff from all levels of the hierarchy. For example, a staff person who is nonmanagerial, but a key player in the process, might be named the team leader if he or she is a competent worker who is concerned about the problems that are being addressed. This provides a clear signal that everyone, not just managers, should engage in work analysis.

Authority Vested in Quality Improvement Teams

As noted in Chapter Two, TQM should not be confused with participatory democracy. Management is not ceding its responsibility for directing an organization; the final decisions on how work is done remain with management (Harrington, 1987). However, TQM does require that management enable workers to describe how the work is actually accomplished and to propose improvements in work processes. According to *The Team Handbook,* "Effective leaders share their responsibilities with other team members, and trust their groups to arrive at the best answer, giving team members a chance to succeed or make mistakes on their own. They understand that the lessons members learn from experience are stronger and last longer than those from having the leader telling them what to do" (Scholtes and others, 1988, p. 3-9).

Naturally, if management does not believe that workers are capable of accurately analyzing work processes, and do not give credence to the analyses prepared by workers, staff will stop analyzing work. Similarly, if management does not accept a reasonable proportion of the improvement ideas suggested by staff (at least on a pilot-experiment basis), staff will stop proposing improvements. Therefore, while management must still make the final decision on how to organize the workplace, if they are not willing to listen and learn from staff, they might as well not bother with TQM. They will fail at it. The authority given to improvement teams is the authority to collect and analyze data on work processes, to identify problems, and to propose improved work processes for management approval. The responsibility placed on management is to utilize these data and proposed improvements in organizing work.

Integrating TQM into the Management Structure

This leads to the final point of organizing for TQM: the need to make it a part of your routine management structure. Eventually the initial improvement teams you began with should be seen as the normal way of thinking and working, rather than some kind of special case. As we noted above, when new assignments are given, or in the routine procedure of carrying out an old task, staff will continuously describe and attempt to improve the conduct of that task. Management should constantly ask the following questions in reviewing and directing work.

1. Who is the customer?
2. What does the customer want and how was this ascertained?
3. Who are the suppliers and what is being done to communicate needs to them and to obtain higher-quality supplies in a more timely manner?
4. What is the current level of performance of this task?
5. How are you attempting to improve the process, and, consequently, the level of performance?

Integrating TQM into your management structure means, in part, training your managers to constantly ask these questions and to build incentive systems that reward those who are good at doing this. In government, most organizational heroes are those who are best at responding to pressure-packed fire drills. Government will always need people who are agile enough to turn around on a dime and perform at a pace that responds to the concerns of political leaders and the media. However, government also needs to reward people who get the work done and deliver services effectively, so that emergencies are reduced or eliminated, people who are willing to fight in the trenches in the long battle for continuous improvement.

TQM requires patience and tenacity. These are traditional American values, but they are less present in this world of sound bites, fast food, and short attention spans. Focusing on your own work can, at first, be tedious and mundane. It takes a while to develop an appreciation for the beauty and subtlety of small improvements. Just as a traditional Japanese garden contains many intricate, beautiful small details, so too does a work process that has been subjected to many years of continuous improvement. It takes much time and patience to pare down and eliminate waste from a complex and cumbersome work process. Currently, this is not seen as an important aspect of public management, as the focus of management attention is on policy, legislation, and budget formulation. Infusing the value of continuous improvement throughout your organization is not simple and will take many years. It is nothing less than a change in culture, consciously generated and transmitted.

Utilizing Supplier and Customer Analysis to Improve Work Processes

Since the customer determines quality, we need to start our analysis with customers. In Chapter Three, we discussed the task of analyzing customer needs and your requirements of your own suppliers. The worksheets in Exhibits 3.1 and 3.2 were designed to get you started on this process. This section provides some further guidance on how to conduct supplier and customer analyses.

Working with Your Supplier

First you must identify what you need from your supplier, which requires that you have a solid knowledge of your work processes. Then you must develop procedures for communicating those needs to suppliers. Every task you perform begins with a set of materials, documents, concepts, or data: your supplies. If your supplies are inadequate it is likely your product will be inadequate. The first step in deciding what you need from your supplier is conceptual: learn to view your work as the midpoint of a production process beginning with your supplier and ending with your customer.

Let us look at an example. Most public managers have had the fairly unpleasant experience of trying to hire a staff person under civil service rules. In the process of bringing your new person on board, you are "supplied" with a hiring process governed by an internal personnel office and/or a central civil service organization such as the federal Office of Personnel Management. The process you must follow, the form of the position description, the job announcement, the interview and review process, and sometimes the decision on whom you are certified to hire is governed by a complex and often cumbersome set of rules. Most experienced civil servants know that by working with the personnel office the rules can be applied in a less rigid manner than if that office is ignored. In essence you are working with your supplier to adjust your "supply"—the rules governing hiring to better fit your work—to ensure that you can hire an appropriate person for your position.

TQM asks you to take this essential process one step further. Work with the personnel office to try to set up a more effective system for doing all your hires, speeding up the recruitment and selection process. This does not remove the need to work informally with the personnel office, but it does provide for a working relationship that begins from a "higher" base. Explore with the personnel office the steps involved in getting a position approved. How many people must approve a new position? What type of information do they need to make their decision? What type of process delays are typical? In a real sense, when we are trying to hire someone, we are both suppliers and customers of the personnel staff. Perhaps the form accompanying the position description can be better crafted to ease acceptance of the position. Perhaps the personnel office can combine or shorten some approval processes.

Ronald Brand undertook such a process at the Underground Tank Office. In state and federal agencies, consultants are often the biggest and most consistently used suppliers; thus, it is particularly important that you set up a process whereby your consultants are kept well informed of your needs. One feature of newer federal agencies like the EPA, the Department of Housing and Urban Development (HUD), and the Department of Energy are multipurpose mission contracts. These agencies were all formed during an era of great sensitivity to the size of the federal workforce and have fairly small staffs when compared to their functions. One way to assist limited staff is to use and work with a contractor or to use a mission contract— contracts let with large analytical consulting firms and designed to provide specialized support to federal agencies. These contracts are typically for several million dollars a year and often provide an office more workyears of contracted staff support than it has in its own organization.

When staff in the Office of Underground Storage Tanks (OUST) want to assign a job to the mission contractor, they write a task order that goes to the EPA's central contract office, and, if it is deemed appropriate for the contract, is then forwarded to the contractor. This formal process is usually augmented by an informal process of direct contact with the contractor to explain the nature of the assignment. Brand's staff discovered that this communication process was not working particularly well and that they were not receiving the type of products (or supplies) they expected from their contractors. This resulted in rework and missed deadlines for both parties. They decided to structure their direct contact with the consultants by adding a formal planning meeting to the beginning of every new task order. Their consultants were encouraged to tell them the truth about the feasibility of OUST assignments and provide the program with a realistic assessment of what they would be able to get for the money they were spending and for the time allocated for the work. Although adding this step did not end all of their problems with their contractors, it did result in a significant improvement in the quality of the work that they received. Exhibit 5.2, a sample letter describing (in detail) OUST's needs, illustrates how the program worked with their contractors to improve service to their customers.

Deciding what you need from your supplier is an interactive, iterative process. You look at what you are producing and how you shape the supplies you are given into a final product. You work with your suppliers to see what they are capable of producing and what they will need to subcontract. You want to avoid a formal process where you just drop some specifications into a long detailed document that you ship off to your sup-

Exhibit 5.2. Sample Letter Describing Needs.

SUBJECT: Coordination on OUST Project Work
FROM: Division Director
TO: Project Officer, ABC Inc.

As promised, here are my follow-up notes from our meeting on Monday, September 11, at ABC. They follow in no particular order:

- First, and most important, I appreciate the opportunity for our respective teams to sit down together and discuss what we're doing and how we can do it better. I perceive that we are still at the "polite stage"; I expect that more candor will come as we build trust and confidence among members of the team. It may be intimidating to speak up in the presence of so many people and their managers. But we got off to a good start, and we'll keep working at it.

- *What we want from ABC:* Simply put, we want ABC to be a full partner in the project work. ABC staff should push back on OUST anytime they don't understand the assignment. Of necessity, work assignments may be written in a general way. However, it is *very* important that you know what we're trying to do and why. I urge you to charge your staff to push back on us if it is not perfectly clear. We don't want to waste our money and your time trying to carry out vague assignments.

- "Pushing back" also means we want the benefit of your experience, judgment, and creativity when it comes to designing projects and carrying them out. There will be times when our direction is flawed; we are not perfect. Rather than politely doing the wrong thing, I want ABC to argue with us a little bit, bringing to our attention the problems you foresee. Ultimately the EPA will make the decision, but in doing so I want to be sure we have listened to and considered your ideas and concerns. It would be wrong to presume that your task is merely to follow our instructions, however vague or ill advised. As a full partner you have the right and the responsibility to raise a flag when you see a problem. We have the responsibility to listen.

- *Radical solutions:* Our office places a premium on innovative approaches to the solving of public-sector problems. It is both refreshing and challenging to be able to define new ways of doing business in EPA and the states. In the franchising and total quality management work we have done, OUST has drawn freely from private-sector parallels in shaping our program. We have only scratched the surface in this area. We look to you for fresh, new ideas.

- *Amnesty:* We are trying to foster a work environment where everyone feels safe to identify problems and barriers to our success. We have agreed that no area of our work (policy, procedures, administrative details) is exempt from scrutiny and that anyone can speak up. I want to make it clear that we extend these rights and responsibilities to our colleagues at ABC as well.

- *Keeping ABC informed of OUST decisions:* You mentioned that you often do not learn of OUST management decisions that affect your work until too late. I'd like to explore with you the specifics of this problem so we can fix it.

Sincerely,
cc: PSD Staff
Division Director

plier. The communication process should attempt to facilitate honesty, listening, and learning, so it is essential to avoid the symbolic posturing that often characterizes interorganizational communication in the public sector. Frequent and informal contact is important. You are attempting to create an ongoing, long-term working relationship: a partnership based on shared areas of self-interest.

Analyzing Customer Needs and Using Them in Setting Goals

When you communicate with your suppliers, you are taking on the role of the aggressive customer trying to make sure that the goods and services you are buying truly meet your needs. Although you need to take responsibility for communicating with your suppliers, it is better for the supplier to initiate contact with the customer. The operational definition of quality involves meeting or exceeding customer requirements and evaluating needs and expectations. If you do not communicate with your customers, it is difficult to tell what they need.

Some public managers find it difficult to think of citizens and clients as customers. Often, one problem is that those receiving a service do not pay for it directly; theoretically, we are all taxpayers who pay for government services, but the process of payment is far removed from delivery. Another problem is that since many government services are monopolies many government employees believe that the "customer" has no choice but to shop at our store. A final conceptual problem is that citizens who are potential customers of our programs may have contradictory needs. Which part of the public is my customer? If I focus my resources on one segment, as a private firm might do as a normal part of their marketing strategy, I may get in trouble with another segment.

With all these problems, what is the utility of the concept of customer in the public sector? First, it focuses public managers outside their organization where much of their attention belongs. Second, it connotes an exchange relationship, and, even if cash is not the medium of exchange, it helps reinforce the fact that the clients of public programs are entitled to excellent service.

This brings us back to the fundamental issue of identifying customer needs. The best place to begin the process is to rediscover the basic purpose of the program you are working in. What was this program designed to do? Whom are you trying to assist? Whose behavior are you trying to influence? What facility or service are you attempting to put in place and whom is it designed to serve? If you are building a highway or issuing driver's licenses, you must always set priorities and target your efforts toward some group. Once you decide who this group is, you must engage in a constant dialogue with them to identify, understand, better define, and possibly even anticipate their changing needs. We recognize that these targeting decisions are subject to frequent change. In a dynamic, volatile issue area, the highest-priority customers can change with almost dizzying speed.

Your job in assessing customer needs is not to consider them as if you are unconstrained. Instead, you should communicate with your customers about the type of environment in which you are operating and in spite of constraints do the best job you can to match what you deliver with what they need. We are not saying that serving customers means giving them everything they ask for. The private sector certainly does not do that: the person who can afford a Toyota Corolla but wants a Rolls Royce is going to have to make do with the Toyota. However, to the extent possible, a customer analysis will enable you to direct the resources you can obtain to the needs expressed by the customer. Let us look at a manufacturing example. In some Japanese cars you see little plastic cutouts where drivers can place coffee cups. These cupholders probably cost little to manufacture. However, to anyone who drinks coffee in the car during the morning rush hour, this small detail may make the experience of driving to work more pleasurable, and at least a bit drier. While there is a chance that such an improvement might be made without talking to customers, the odds of discovering this easy-to-satisfy need are much higher if you actually talk to customers and observe their behavior.

Contrasting the motor vehicle departments of a mid-Atlantic state and a certain northeastern state provides a public-sector example of assessing customer needs. Customers seeking to renew their licenses in a suburban area in the northeastern state arrive at a too small parking lot in a nondescript office complex. They walk into a huge facility where the first step is to get into a long line labeled "information." They are directed to a number of forms that they fill out while standing in another line labeled "license renewals." The rest of the experience goes downhill from there, ending two hours later (if they do everything right) with a promise that the license will be mailed in about three weeks.

In contrast, the mid-Atlantic state provides its customers with a different experience. A storefront license renewal facility is housed in a major shopping center. While your friend goes to windowshop, you walk into a clean, modern, moderate-sized facility, sign a registration book, help yourself to a cup of coffee, and sit in a waiting area and read a magazine. You do not get very far into the magazine because in about three minutes your name is called and a person sitting at a computer terminal takes your license, asks you some questions, and directly inputs your responses into a computer. That same person administers your eye exam, takes your fee, and lowers a machine to take a picture of you. You go back to read the magazine you had started before, and in another three minutes you are handed your completed picture-i.d. license and join your friend shopping at the record store. The entire experience takes ten minutes, half of which involves reading a magazine. You do not stand in any lines and you walk out with the license in your pocket.

The people who designed the second process had learned that their customers do not like to wait. But they also learned that if they had to wait they would rather be sitting than standing. Waiting time seemed less of a burden if they were given some refreshments and provided with reading material. They also found out that people do not like to fill out forms, and they knew that filling out forms could be eliminated by directly entering the data into the computer. Since the data on the form eventually had to be entered into the computer anyway, doing it during the registration process did not add to the cost of processing. In fact, since the customer was asked to check the license before signing it, the cost of checking the accuracy of the data input was reduced as well. Finally, the staff in the mid-Atlantic state found out that customers who had waited (even a short period of time) to renew their license felt better about the wait and in fact about the whole renewal process if they were able to leave with their license. By providing the license on the spot, money was saved in processing and mailing the licenses and the number of errors made were reduced.

This example illustrates how customer preferences can be used in setting goals and influencing operational decisions. There is little question that the mid-Atlantic state's license renewal process was perceived by customers to be higher in quality than the northeastern state's. It is also quite likely that the cost of delivering this higher-quality service was no greater (and possibly less) than the lower-quality service. Funds were saved in processing and mailing licenses, checking the license accuracy, not printing application forms, and eliminating the need to staff an information booth. Customer needs become a guide for designing the service and can also be a way of measuring its success. Public organizations do not have a profit-and-loss statement as a measure of success, but customer satisfaction serves as an excellent substitute.

Analyzing Your Own Work

When you mention waste to most people, they picture workers loafing at their desks or machines, reading newspapers, or chatting about the ballgame or tonight's dinner. But this type of waste is infinitesimal compared to the waste in the work. This is what Deming means when he says, "They are only doing their best." If you have a system that makes managers redo the budget four times or workers retype materials five times or applicants resubmit forms two times, that is all waste. But notice that everyone involved is working very hard; they are not loafing; they are doing what the system is making them do. The waste is in the work.

Describing Your Work

Working with suppliers and customers is critical to quality improvement; so too is analyzing the work of your own organization, and, in fact, your own personal role in the work processes of your branch, division, or office. Before attempting to improve performance, you must first be able to describe it. What are the steps in the work process? Who does what when? How long do discrete work activities take to complete? How often are these activities interrupted? When is work delayed? What are the causes of delays? How much variation is there in performance levels? Why does the same activity take one day to complete at one time, twenty minutes at another time, and forty minutes at a third time? As a manager, does your work contribute to variation in the time needed to complete tasks? For the specific process that you are concerned about, you need to ask: Is my direction timely? Is my in-basket the biggest cause of delays in the process? How do I use my time?

Another way to look at or describe work was demonstrated by Bill Conway in his training program and is explained in his book *The Quality Secret* (1992). We have found that this is a useful way to help people identify waste as a step in the improvement process. The brief names for each category are frequently adopted by everyone and greatly facilitate the communication process, both internally and among suppliers and customers.

Value-Added Work. This is work that adds a benefit for the customer. In most organizations, less than 30 percent of the time spent working involves performing some value-added work. Some examples include

1. Reducing some key information in an eighty-page manual to a two-sided laminated card that the worker can carry into the field for use when working with soil emissions at a site
2. Designing a form so that the citizens filling it out can get it right the first time
3. Developing a Spanish language booklet so that people who do not understand or read English well can understand and comply with the rules that apply to their business

Necessary but Not Value-Added Work. All organizations need infrastructure and must have processes in place that relate to their own maintenance. These tasks do not directly add value for an external customer, but without this work no one would be around to perform value-added work. Examples of this type of work might include developing the organization's budget, getting contracts out, transferring personnel, arranging for desks and telephones, and maintaining an organization's computers. We have found it helpful to view all of these activities as setup time, that is, preliminary steps to the program work of your agency or branch. As such, you want to minimize the time that people in your organization have to spend doing such work, so they can do more value-added work to serve your clientele. Some examples of this are

1. Reducing the elapsed time for preparing the budget from five weeks to two weeks and the workdays required from five person-months to two person-months
2. Eliminating the complexity and opportunities for error and rework so that things like travel authorizations and vouchers take up less work time, freeing up more time for people to do value-added work
3. Drastically cutting back the material to be prepared and submitted for renewing a grant in recognition of the fact that the paperwork does not improve the program services funded by the grant

Rework. This is work that does not meet the customer's requirement and must be redone. Some examples are

1. A memo, report, or presentation that is redone three, four, five, or more times
2. Inquiries from customers or suppliers about unclear directions or specifications, each call requiring a reexplanation of what we should have communicated more clearly in the first place
3. A meeting room or time that is changed at the last minute for a conference so ten people have to return to their offices or march over to another building
4. A major report that takes months to complete and is then

bounced by the boss, who paid no attention to it until two days before it was due, which results in lots of late nights and weekend rework

We emphasize the frequency and variety of rework because in most organizations (and for most of us as individuals) rework makes up about 30 to 40 percent of our work. We can improve our work processes so that *people can get the work done right the first time.*

Unnecessary Work. This is work for which there is no customer, or, even if there is a customer, the work is unnecessary. Some examples are

1. Just-in-case backup files or data runs: in case someone asks, we've got the information
2. Reports for which no feedback or indication of purpose is ever received
3. Status reports and exhortations that the personnel, budget, or facilities offices get the boss to sign and send out to the field in the belief that they will improve performance

Sometimes an organization churns out reports, forms, and data out of habit. The appropriation still exists, the organization is still in place, and the product marches on.

Not Working. What we are concerned with here are situations where the worker is ready to work but is delayed or prevented from doing so by the organization's work system. Examples include computers that are down, copier machines that constantly jam, a task force that cannot meet because there is no conference room available, ten people waiting for the boss so that a meeting can start, and cases where a supplier fails to get material in on time so that the next persons in the process can do their part of the job.

Analyzing Performance

How many meetings have you sat through where there was no organized development or presentation of the problem, no description of the pertinent processes, no identification of the obstacles to success, or no realistic data on current levels of performance? In meetings like this, people usually just talk around the problem, offering lots of opinions but few facts or data. Also, the meetings usually end with no clear agreement on any of the issues or the appropriate next steps.

Assessing your current level of performance requires that you dissect the work processes in your organization and in your own workday in order to identify constituent elements. Work can be broken down at a variety of levels, depending on the problem and action that you are considering. If you discover that people are having a difficult time getting through to your staff on the telephone, for example, you might attempt to obtain the following information to determine how incoming phone calls are handled by your staff:

- How many times does the phone ring before it is picked up?
- What greeting is used?
- How frequently are callers placed on hold?
- How long are callers kept waiting?
- How are messages given to your staff? Who does this work, and how long does it take for the staff to receive the message?
- How are return calls assigned to staff by management? Are deadlines given?

Each discrete element of work can be identified, described, or measured. This is an effort to build a foundation for developing improved processes. We frequently find that the people involved in a work process disagree about what actually takes place. They either make incorrect assumptions about what other people are doing or are unable to fit their activities into a broader context. Later in this chapter, we will discuss the development of flow charts as a useful device for describing work processes. A consensus can often be developed about how work is currently performed by putting all of the participants who are involved in a single work process in the same room and asking them to describe the steps that they go through and recording their answers on a flow chart.

People work within a system, usually created by management. When staff are not achieving expected results, the probability is about 85 percent that the problem is in the system (Deming, 1986). An important part of this analysis involves determining the amount and range of variation in the process. For example, three different offices may respond to controlled correspondence with the following results: office A: 99 percent completed by deadline; office B: 80 percent completed by deadline; and office C: 50 percent completed by deadline. If these offices produce results like this consistently, over time, then they have systems that produce 50, 80, and 99 percent on-time completions. We would have to look inside their systems to determine the causes of the variation. In one such case that we encountered, the process on such correspondence involved so many steps, approvals, and logging entries that getting the request to the person who had to prepare the answer used up eight of the ten days available to her to research and write the responses. What could the employee do? The worker was working within the system that management had created.

Too often in cases like this management simply "yells" at people: they hold a meeting, send out a memo, or report back on how badly each unit is doing. In doing this, management is simply telling staff to "do better" without providing the means. The tools described below, and the examples that follow, should help provide a way to do better.

Tools of Work Analysis

A number of simple statistical, brainstorming, and presentation tools are available for analyzing work. According to *The Team Handbook,* "These tools help your team visualize a process, pinpoint problems, find their causes, and determine solutions. They also provide a way to evaluate proposed changes" (Scholtes and others, 1988, p. 2-18). They build an understanding of the systemic elements and discrete steps involved in performing work. Although a variety of tools have been developed, we present five that we believe are the most useful: (1) the fishbone, or cause-and-effect diagram, (2) the pareto diagram and bar chart, (3) the flow chart, (4) the run chart, and (5) the control chart. You may find it useful to adapt these tools to the particular requirements of your organization.

Most problems are first perceived as specific incidents. A report is late, an application is incomplete, a letter contains errors, or a request for service is not answered. As these occur more frequently, managers start to get more upset and the people involved are told, "We've got to do something about that problem. Fix it." At this point, most organizations and supervisors start randomly suggesting solutions, such as training, additional management controls, and adding more staff. A useful way to take advantage of the desire to solve the problem is to use a tool developed by Dr. Kaoru Ishikawa, known as the "cause-and-effect" diagram, or the *fishbone.*

The purpose of using the fishbone is to determine the causes of an undesired effect before jumping to ill-advised solutions. Start by sketching a fishbone diagram on a flip chart or blackboard, as shown in Figure 5.1.

Then write a specific description of the problem in the "head" of the fishbone, for example:

It takes too long to hire new people.
Requests for information are not answered.
Requests for information are not answered on time.
The cost of analyzing lab samples is too high.
Cases are inadequately documented.

Avoid mixing two or more different kinds of problems in one problem statement. That is why "requests not answered" is distinguished from "requests not answered on time." In considering problems, managers tend to mix up quality issues with issues of productivity or cost. Although there may be a connection between these problems, it is important to focus on only one as the group does a fishbone. You may wish to add other categories, but we have found the four shown in Figure 5.1 to be the ones that are most applicable.

After selecting a problem statement, the group brainstorms about possible causes of the problem, which are listed on the appropriate bones of the fish (Figure 5.1). In the case of

Figure 5.1. Fishbone Diagram.

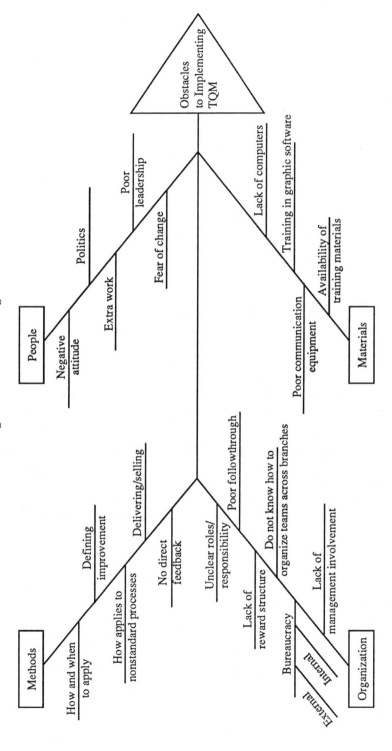

the "requests for information are not answered" problem, for example, the group might list causes such as

Requests not sent to right person
Requests not logged in
Don't know how to prepare answer
No word processors available
I'm already overloaded with work
We hate to do these

It is important to have people list all of the causes they can think of. Do not list solutions. The purpose of this exercise is to help people decide which causes of the problem are most important, and only after identifying and making those choices can staff work on solutions. Reviewing the causes of particular problems will make it clear that different causes require different solutions. The fishbone diagram is a useful way to get everyone in the office involved in problem solving. By encouraging your employees to think in these terms, you are developing their ability to think critically about their work environment and to invest in developing avenues for problem solving.

Another useful tool is the *pareto chart*. A pareto chart is a graph that ranks events in order of frequency, duration, or importance. The defining characteristic is that the chart illustrates a ranking. By ranking the frequency of events, the pareto chart plainly illustrates which factors or problems require the majority of your attention. Rather than spend 90 percent of your time working on 10 percent of the problem (all too often the case), the chart helps you focus your attention.

The first step is to gather data on which causes occur most frequently, are most significant, or incur the greatest costs. In our experience, however, data on organizational operations are rarely available, especially in the early days of a quality improvement program. Management should initiate efforts to begin gathering those data, and in the meantime, the frontline workers should be asked to rank the causes that they believe are the most important. They can do this by voting on the causes, which will create a ranking based on the group's perceptions. After developing a fishbone diagram on the causes of late budget reports, we might produce a ranking such as the one in Figure 5.2.

The group then agrees to work on the first or second cause that got the most votes. If the first cause is one that is beyond the control of your organization, save it for later and work on the number two or three cause. Focusing on the most important cause possible has three additional effects. The essence of the pareto principle is that 80 percent of the effect is caused by 20 percent of the events, whether they are defects,

Figure 5.2. Pareto Chart: Reasons for Late Monthly Budget Reports.

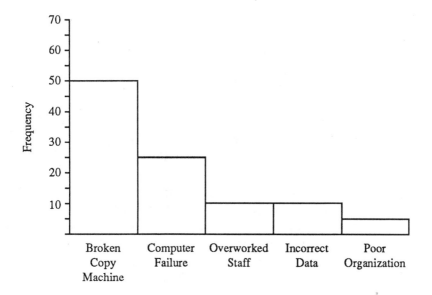

errors, or completions. First, it helps the group to deflect any preconceived or erroneous solutions from the boss or a strong-willed group member. Second, it identifies the work that should be done once inroads have been made on the first and second causes. Finally, it reduces or eliminates one cause of a problem, so that you may get information about other causes of the same problem.

A third important tool in analyzing work processes is the *flow chart*. The flow chart is a step-by-step presentation of a sequence of events involved in a particular process. By identify-ing the various steps in a large process, you begin to understand the real work. Often, the perception of what takes place in a process is very different from reality. Constructing a flow chart can help you get closer to reality by identifying the actual steps involved in a process. Flow charts are also useful in identifying who and what are involved in a process. Finally, a flow chart can help identify areas where the process can be improved.

You may have created flow charts in the past. If so, you probably used one or more of the following ways:

1. You developed a logical flow chart from your personal knowledge and memory or from written procedures.
2. You put it together with a few other analysts from staff offices.
3. You met with two or three supervisors involved in the process and attempted to describe it.

The difference with the quality approach to creating a flow chart is that you bring together the people who actually perform the tasks you want to describe. We recommend that you have the group identify all of the steps in the process and list each one on a separate piece of paper. Putting them on Post-It notes that can then be stuck on a flip chart or even the wall works well for this. We have found that it is best not to attempt to put the steps in order at this stage. Once all the steps are listed, then ask the group to arrange them in sequence, which increases the chance that you will create a flow chart that is closer to the process as it is genuinely carried out. It also helps all the people involved to better understand the entire process. Flow charts are often used in problem solving when you want to understand how work actually gets done and where improvement in the process is needed.

One of the most important steps in developing a flow chart is identifying the process that you wish to analyze. For example, do you want to describe the process involved in implementing a specific project or the process involved in setting up the project?

Once you have specified the process, begin to break it down into the individual steps involved, and then identify the sequence of events. Next, determine the nature of each step. For example, is it a decision or an operation? Putting data in the computer may be viewed as filing. Use a different symbol in your chart for each type of step; then plot these steps sequentially. You may also want to indicate the amount of time a step takes to complete. Figure 5.3 is a flow chart of the process of making coffee in the morning. While this may seem fairly simplistic, think of all the possible extra steps that you might encounter in performing the tasks outlined. The coffee pot might be dirty and need to be cleaned. You might be out of filters; the freezer with your coffee beans might be in the basement. If all of these obstacles are removed, making coffee can be done with greater speed and with higher quality.

The flow chart provides you with a starting point for work analysis. You may find that several people have added a step to the process. In our example you grind your own coffee beans, which improves the flavor of the coffee, but adds a step to the process. If you have a machine that supplies its own water, you eliminate a step from the process. Since you can only improve from where you are, the flow chart developed in this way, with the workers, gives you a good baseline from which to make improvements. With the flow chart, you can identify unnecessary steps and those steps that slow the process down. Now you can make use of the fishbone to determine obstacles, causes of delay, or poor performance at a particular step in the process.

A fourth useful tool is the *run chart*. A run chart is an illustration of measurements taken at regular intervals of time.

Figure 5.3. Sample Flow Chart.

Symbol	Visual Representation	Definition
Diamond	◇	Decision
Square	☐	Control/Inspection
Circle	◯	Operation
Arrow	⬆	Movement/Transfer
"D"	◖	Delay
Triangle	△	File

If you use this time-oriented analysis, these charts can be important tools for monitoring performance or for identifying trends. By tracking an event for an extended period of time, you can tell whether important changes occur and, if so, at what point in time they occurred.

Run charts can be used with any data that can be collected over time, including those that describe how often an activity takes place, how much of a product is produced, or how often a service is delivered. Run charts are most effectively used in the early stages of the problem-solving process when it is important to understand the level of performance or to graphically make trends visible. They are much more effective than lists of figures in a tabular form.

Run charts can also be used to compare the progress of two different events over time. For example, if you wish to determine which method for processing service requests is most effective, chart, over a period of time, the number of requests processed by each method. By comparing the two charts, it is possible to determine if one method is more consistent or more effective than the other.

To construct a run chart, begin by selecting an activity, process, or other event you wish to analyze over time. Select an appropriate interval of time for recording the frequency of the activity, such as daily, weekly, or monthly. Once the data have been collected, place the time intervals on the horizontal axis and the quantity of the activity on the vertical axis. By plotting the number of activities identified for each time interval, you can now see the trends of the specified activity over time (see Figure 5.4).

The fifth tool is the *control chart* (see Figure 5.5). Used appropriately and effectively, a control chart can be a useful statistical method for making constant improvements. It is basically a run chart with an upper and lower limit set from the process average. Control charts are used for data that either can be measured (for example, lengths, volume, temperature, pressure, voltage) or counted (for example, defective components, typographical errors, incomplete applications) (Walton, 1986).

Figure 5.4. Run Chart: Service Requests Processed by Method.

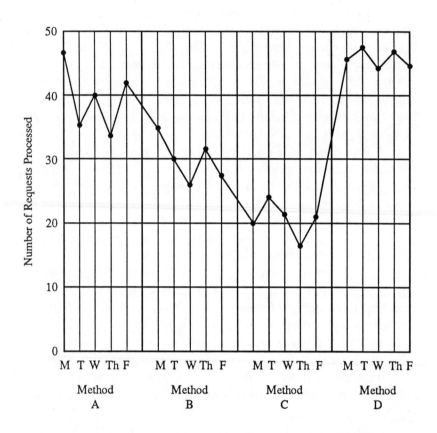

Figure 5.5. Sample Control Chart.

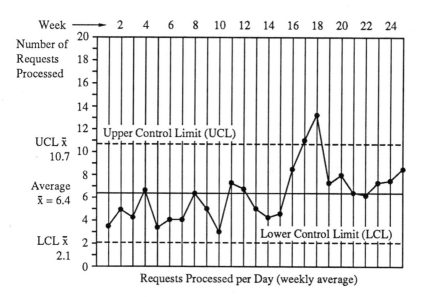

Control charts provide pictures that identify "outliers." Since a fundamental method of quality analysis is to identify variation in performance, the control chart can help management "see" variation and thus improve the system by eliminating the common causes that lead to particular variations. In many organizations, people do not know their current or past level of performance or the range of variation in their performance for their key processes. How many rejects do they have, how many applications returned, paychecks with errors, incomplete inspection reports, and so on? How can the manager make a commitment or estimate what resources she will need if the daily rejection rate is running 38 percent, 2 percent, 17 percent, 29 percent, and 7 percent? This system is not in statistical control. It would be better if her operation's rejection rate averaged 18 to 20 percent a day because she could then predict what would happen and plan accordingly. Once the system is under statistical control, performance is easier to predict, providing management with a strong base for making fundamental changes and improvements.

The development and use of control charts is more complex than is appropriate to discuss here. You should draw on statisticians from your agency or a nearby university for early help on this. For those who would like to learn more themselves, training in statistical process control is appropriate. An excellent basic book on this subject is *Understanding Statistical Process Control* (Wheeler and Chambers, 1992).

The Case of the Seven-Month Hiring Process

To illustrate work analysis, this chapter concludes by presenting the imaginary case of "Dorothy Oz and the Drug Education Program."

Homer Bart Cosby, the new governor of the state of Flatexmass, had just come into office after promising to establish a massive drug education program. He created a new cabinet level position and on January 15 appointed a commissioner of drug education programs. On January 20, the new commissioner, Bill Simpson, was given (on six-month detail) a five-person staff from the existing Department of Mental Health and received an allocation to hire 100 new staff people. On January 24, Governor Cosby charged Commissioner Simpson with the goal of launching a massive drug education program in 100 days. By May 1, the governor expected to see a visible, aggressive new program.

On January 25, the commissioner met with his five-person staff and asked if anyone had experience in hiring people. Reluctantly, Dorothy Oz volunteered that she had gotten her start in government working for the Department of Mental Health's personnel office. Since that time she had received a master's degree and had developed expertise in mass communication and education, but she could lend a hand and at least help hire a personnel director for the new organization.

On January 26, Dorothy met with the Flatexmass Department of Government Personnel (DGP) and discussed the need to create a small human resources office for the new drug education organization, as well as to hire a personnel director to head that office so that people could be hired to operate the agency's program. DGP told Ms. Oz that there was no quick way to staff this organization and that the governor's 100-day goal was simply not feasible for a new organization. On average, the normal process for creating a new position took a total of nine months from start to finish. According to DGP the following steps requiring the following amount of time needed to be taken:

1. Review and approval by DGP of the position description submitted by the agency (one month).
2. Advertisement of the position (minimum of thirty days).
3. Review and rank by DGP of applications (two months from the close of the announcement).
4. Interview of the top five candidates by the agency (one month).
5. Once the top choice has been made by the hiring agency, a "request to hire" justification form must be submitted and approved by DGP (one month).
6. Once the request to hire form has been approved by DGP,

an "authorization to hire" form must be drafted, approved, signed and sent by DGP to the hiring agency (one month).

Dorothy listened to the presentation with alarm. She observed that, when faced with a similar problem in Kansas, the staff had used the techniques of total quality management and hired fifty new staff people in five weeks. The DGP staff observed that Dorothy should realize that she was no longer in Kansas and her goal could not be achieved. Ms. Oz was a determined public manager, however, and after meeting with Commissioner Simpson, she suggested that he and Governor Cosby meet with Commissioner Lethargy of the Department of Government Personnel and challenge him to reduce the hiring process from seven to two months. On February 1 this meeting took place and, at 8:00 A.M. on Saturday, February 2, Dorothy Oz met with an unhappy group of DGP staff to attempt to design a streamlined hiring process.

Dorothy brought a box of donuts to the meeting and, after ensuring that everyone had a little sugar in their systems, decided to give the group a quick forty-five-minute introduction to TQM's core concepts and tools. Her point was that the group had a terrific opportunity to revisit and improve a process that all of them found frustrating. The first step she suggested was that the group brainstorm and develop a detailed flow chart of the entire hiring process, including the approximate amount of time each step took. Figure 5.6 is a copy of the flow chart they developed.

When the group looked at and discussed the flow chart, it gradually became obvious that a number of steps were not needed; that a great deal of review was unnecessary; and that a lot of time was wasted transporting forms, logging them in, and waiting for senior staff to review them. With the exception of the legal requirement to post job announcements for thirty days, there was leeway to eliminate much of the time. One member of the group had obtained a dozen recruitment files and decided to tabulate the amount of time the forms sat in the various offices of DGP. Table 5.1 provides the data that she found.

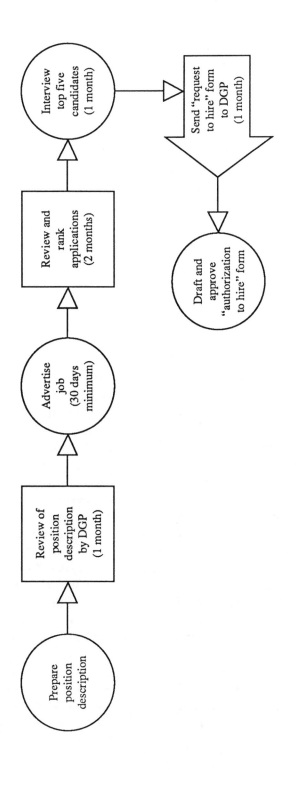

Figure 5.6. Hiring Process.

Table 5.1. Amount of Time in Various DGP Offices.

Office	Total Process Time (in days)	Number of Cases	Average Process Time (in days)
Mail room	400	12	33.3
Position control	250	12	20.8
Rating division	945	12	78.8
Agency liaison	25	12	2.1
Deputy commissioner	905	12	75.4
Commissioner	24	12	2
		Total Average	210.4

Ms. Oz suggested that to help focus their work they ought to first look at those offices that took the most time to review and process position forms. To facilitate this analysis, she drew the pareto diagram that appears as Figure 5.7, which graphically illustrated that two units in particular seemed to be bottlenecks: the rating division and the office of the deputy commissioner for operations. The group decided to do flow charts of the review process in each of those offices.

They found, in both cases, that two specific processes caused excessive delays: the time it took to open and log in the mail and the time it took to get the deputy commissioner (D.C.) to sign a position package. On average, position packages were shipped from the rating division to the deputy commissioner's office for signature seventy-three days before they were sent to the agency liaison office for transmittal back to the hiring organization. It took an average of fifty days before the package was logged in at the D.C.'s office.

A recommendation for the D.C. was usually made by her staff within three days, but it then sat in her in-box for an average of nineteen days before signature. The form was logged out in one day and then delivered to the agency liaison office. The group decided to call in the clerical staff of the deputy commissioner's office to brainstorm about the obstacles to quickly logging in position requests. The fishbone diagram in Figure 5.8 illustrates the results of their brainstorming effort.

The fishbone diagram identified a number of potential problems with the logging-in process in the deputy com-

Figure 5.7. Pareto Diagram of Average Review Times for Position Approval.

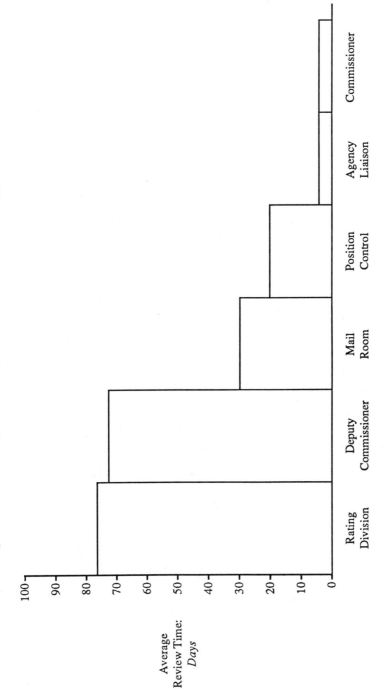

Average
Review Time:
Days

Figure 5.8. Obstacles to Logging Position Requests Quickly.

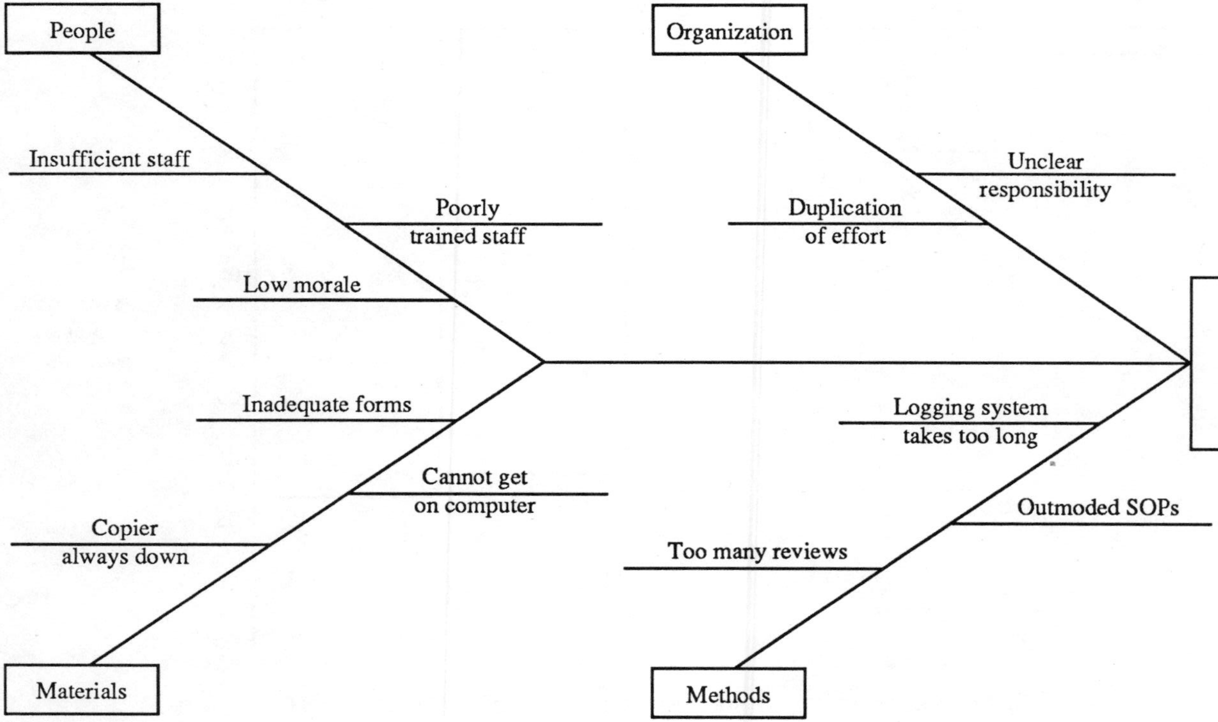

missioner's office. The first was that twelve copies of the position request form were made before they were entered into the log book and assigned a deputy commissioner correspondence control number. The copier was down approximately 65 percent of the time. Because the process took so long, someone almost always had to place a call back to the agency's personnel office to ensure that the request was still valid. Finally, before the D.C. was given the package, the office of position control needed to confirm that the hiring office had the personnel ceiling needed to make the hire.

At this point, Dorothy realized that it was 6:30 P.M. on a Saturday and that everyone was pretty tired. She asked the DGP staff (including clericals from the deputy commissioner's office) to join her on Monday morning for a 7:00 A.M. breakfast meeting to design an improved process for logging in position request packages. Working to remove obstacles that were identified by the fishbone, they designed a new position request package that they believed could be logged in the day it arrived. It included a place on the form where an agency could guarantee they had ceiling available for a specific period of time for the position. The position request itself was to be considered valid until the ceiling authorization expired. Finally, the D.C.'s office reduced their need for copies from twelve to three and asked the hiring agency to supply the package in triplicate (avoiding the need to copy the forms in the D.C.'s office). In one week the clerical staff eliminated their backlog and began to provide position packages to the D.C. the same day they arrived in the office.

While Ms. Oz was happy with the progress she made in the first few days of her efforts, she had a long way to go if she was to meet the governor's 100-day goal. To save time, she hired a TQM consultant to work with the mail room, while she devoted her attention to the rating division.

The job of the rating division was to make certain that the position description submitted by the hiring agency had the appropriate grade level and position title. To her surprise she discovered that the actual time it took to verify a position description varied a great deal. The chief cause of variation was the degree to which the hiring agency understood the rules governing position descriptions.

For example, for a person to be able to obtain the rank and pay of a first-level supervisor, a position description must include at least three activities that the person directs, and he or she must also coordinate at least three additional activities. When Dorothy asked how widely these rules were publicized, she discovered that it had been twelve years since a *Position Description Guidebook* had been published. By asking people who prepared position descriptions, she learned that position packages submitted by staff who had worked for more than ten years averaged 3 days, while those submitted by newer staff took an average of 104 days. Ms. Oz suggested that the DGP hold a series of one-day training courses, and she discovered by the end of February that the average time it took to review a position package was reduced to five days.

Figure 5.9 is a run chart illustrating the progress made by the rating division after they worked with the suppliers of position packages and improved the quality of the position descriptions they reviewed.

By March 1, Dorothy Oz had stimulated significant improvements in DGP's work processes. Although average processing times improved dramatically (see Table 5.2), it still did not look like she would be able to meet her goal of hiring a substantial proportion of her 100-person ceiling in time to have a program in place by May 1. In addition to DGP's new twenty-five-day review time, the position description had to first be written and then posted for thirty days. Next, prospective employees needed to be interviewed and then selected. Fortunately, Dorothy had sold DGP's deputy commissioner for operations on the advantages of TQM. He decided to set up a special experimental pilot project in expedited hiring, using the new drug program as a test case to see how fast 100 people could be hired. By working closely together, they hired seventy-two people between March 1 and April 15. On May 1, an operating drug education program was ready to launch in summer school programs throughout the state.

Figure 5.9. Run Chart.

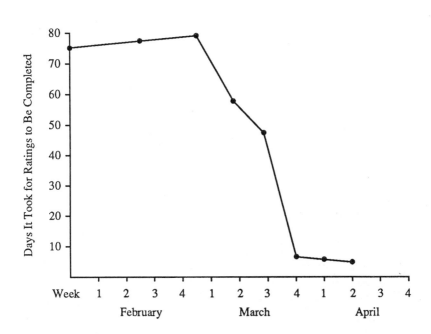

Conclusion: Analyzing Work

We present the preceding imaginary scenario to give you a vivid image of the nuts and bolts of TQM work analysis. Obviously real life is not as neat as this scenario. We also note that the TQM tools used for work analysis in the case are not necessarily always used. As we read the recent literature on TQM, we are struck by what we believe is an overemphasis on specific modes of analysis and the use of particular illustrative tools.

Table 5.2. Processing Times.

Office	Total Review Time (in days)	Number of Cases	Average Review Time (in days)
Mail room	11	10	1.1
Position control	52	10	5.2
Rating division	76	10	7.6
Agency liaison	25	10	2.1
Deputy commissioner	65	10	6.5
Commissioner	24	10	2
		Total Average:	24.5

In our view, all work analysis requires is an honest, factual description and reasonable analysis of work processes, illustrated with flow charts and fishbones or described with lists and text. What is important is developing analytical practices that fit your organization's culture and match the capabilities and preferences of your workers. We have spent most of our careers working with policy offices that are filled with trained analysts. For these staff, simple illustrative charts are not always needed. Rather, what is required are methods for convincing analysts to turn their sharp analytical skills inward to their own operations in order to analyze how they might be improved. The end result will be better product design, more efficient services, and more satisfied customers. The form of analysis is a secondary consideration; performing the function of work analysis is what is really important, and that can be done using a wide variety of formal and informal methods.

CHAPTER 6

Managerial Strategies for
Implementing TQM

You can see in Chapter Five that TQM is a simple, practical, and useful set of activities. Now it is time to discuss concretely how you can bring TQM into your own organization. This chapter begins by describing the role that a manager must play as a change agent to implement TQM. We address a number of basic issues that public managers face when implementing TQM:

- How to get started
- How to deal with all the TQM consultants trying to sell their services
- How to learn about TQM and train your organization
- How to defend your use of TQM with your fellow managers and organizational superiors
- How to develop incentives for employees to work within a TQM framework
- How to implement TQM through your own actions, even without commitment from the top of your organization
- How to recruit your managers and employees to TQM
- How to establish the credibility of the new management system and develop a core group of TQM adherents

Being a Change Agent for TQM

By now you are aware that TQM is more than a collection of charts and slogans. You need to make the whole organization customer driven and enable your suppliers and workers to get things right the first time. But, if your organization is going to successfully adopt the TQM approach to working, it is essential to understand the central role played by managers in implementing TQM. Most of the books on quality management discuss the importance of commitment from an organization's top managers. This type of commitment is difficult to get in industry, and even more difficult to get from politicians. Fortunately, it is possible to implement TQM in any part of an organization, as long as it has its own tasks and at least some capacity for independent action.

The manager's role is key. First, he or she must learn about TQM and its core concepts. In order to make use of these concepts, a change in management style is required. In particular, the manager needs to allow the people and managers doing the work to think through and implement improvements in work processes; second, to convince employees to learn about TQM; and next, to defend the use of it to outsiders in order to ensure that the results of employee-conducted work analysis will be used. This will require a certain amount of courage in rejecting conventional wisdom and accepted practices. Finally, the manager must establish an organizational culture that nurtures and reinforces continuous quality improvement.

Getting Started

What are the concrete steps you as a manager can take to begin implementing TQM? In our view the best way is to ask your organization to begin some quality improvement projects. Then provide the resources needed (in time and training) to learn enough about TQM to complete the assignment.

Cohen and several of his colleagues at Columbia University's Graduate Program in Public Policy and Administration were engaged by New York City's Department of Parks and Recreation to help them implement TQM. The strategy they pursued included the following steps:

1. Each borough and headquarters (HQ) commissioner appointed a quality coordinator from its unit, senior staff with
   clout within the organization.
2. Coordinators attended three briefings to receive instruction on how to identify improvement projects, how to
   initiate and manage improvement teams, and how to do
   work analysis.
3. An all-day meeting was held with the coordinators and their
   bosses to discuss how to manage improvement projects.
4. Each unit was required by the department's commissioner,
   Betsy Gotbaum, to identify three quality improvement
   projects and submit them for approval within ten days.
5. TQM consultants were assigned to each borough and HQ
   unit to provide whatever help was needed to complete these
   first improvement projects. One purpose of the first projects
   was to get some quick victories; the main purpose, however,
   was to teach TQM by doing it. Rather than providing
   abstract training, the commissioner gave an assignment
   that could not be completed unless the staff understood
   TQM. This motivated her staff to learn that TQM was not
   just a bunch of wacky ideas but a body of knowledge needed
   in order to complete an important assignment from the
   boss.

     During the first stage of TQM implementation at the
Department of Parks and Recreation, Columbia faculty trained
about twenty-five people in TQM and quality improvement
project management. During the second stage, over 120 employees learned TQM by working on the department's first
twenty-four quality improvement projects. In later phases of
implementation, units are expected to undertake larger numbers of improvement projects (ten to twenty at a time). Key to
getting TQM started was the decision to begin improvement
projects. TQM training took place as it was needed to complete
the commissioner's assignment.

Dealing with TQM Consultants

TQM has created an industry of consultants who give lectures,
hold training courses, and suggest very specific steps for imple-

menting TQM. We have attended quite a number of these training sessions designed to get an organization started on TQM, and we see lots of mistakes being made. First, many sessions do not result in any concrete actions. At a recent session, Brand talked with a number of senior government managers in attendance, who told him that they had been through training and similar sessions three times over the past year. But when he asked them if they had begun any TQM efforts they responded "No" and expressed great frustration.

At another meeting aimed at getting TQM started in an agency, we encountered a team of managers who had been through two days of training. They were wrestling with how to begin their improvement program. The top manager of this organization was new to her position and had recently replaced an authoritarian director who managed in the traditional command and control method. She, however, was clearly from the participative school of management and had told her employees that she wanted to manage and operate in the TQM mode. Most of the time at the meeting was spent on a discussion about setting up a quality council, who should be on it, what its role should be, and so on. When we asked individual managers if they had tried to do any TQM projects in their own work area, the answer was uniformly no—they did not feel ready to plunge into TQM.

We soon discovered that in their step-by-step (consultant-driven) process they had trained only their managers. They felt they had to have a grand plan before they began training the workers and firstline supervisors. Meanwhile, more than a year had passed. Although this may have been a good business practice for the TQM consultants guiding the process, we believe that it is the wrong way to teach managers about TQM.

In another agency we met with a group of TQM facilitators, who had completed training on TQM along with additional training on how to act as facilitators to help teams working on improvement projects. All division employees had also been trained. They were frustrated because they and their management believed that they had to first set up a council and select cross-cutting projects and team members before they could begin. Meanwhile, two months had passed since they had all been trained and they feared that they were rapidly losing what they had learned, because they could not practice it.

We asked if they had been using elements of TQM in their daily work. "If I attended any of the meetings that you and your unit are involved in daily, would I hear words such as customer, value added, let's improve the process?" They agreed that these types of discussions were not occurring. "Doesn't each of you have responsibility for running some type of operation in your division?" Most of them supervised units of from three to fifteen employees; however, it had not occurred to them to apply the principles and tools of TQM to their daily work. Why? The reason is all the emphasis that current training puts on organizing teams, projects, and councils and selecting the highest-priority projects.

We disagree with that approach as a way to start. We believe that TQM can be started with small steps in any organization. Although some facilitation help may be needed, master plans are really out of place at this stage. A rudimentary understanding of the principles and tools of TQM and a willingness to apply them in your daily work, however, *are* needed.

Learning About TQM

How can you get started? Here are a few ways, depending on your preferences. First, if you have little or no knowledge of TQM, we recommend that you do some reading to see what it is all about. Some personal favorites of ours for this beginning phase include the following eight: (1) Deming, *Out of the Crisis;* (2) Walton, *The Deming Management Method;* (3) Scherkenbach, *The Deming Route to Quality and Productivity;* (4) Crosby, *Quality Is Free;* (5) Imai, *Kaizen;* (6) Dobyns and Crawford-Mason, *Quality or Else;* (7) Goldratt and Cox, *The Goal;* and (8) Schonberger, *Building a Chain of Customers.*

These books give an overview but also enough specifics for you to see the potential and problems in beginning to try to apply TQM to your organization. Most of us are dubious about new management approaches. This reading enables you to see if you are interested at all and gives you a head start before you try to convince others to enroll in the effort.

A second method of learning is to talk with others inside

and outside your own organization who have been doing TQM. Do not limit yourself to other government organizations; people in the private sector encounter many of the same barriers that you will, and you can learn from their successes and failures. It will also give you ideas for projects in your own organization.

In general, we have a bias toward learning by doing. Seminars and videos about TQM are less effective than assignments that can only be completed by understanding TQM. In New York City's Department of Parks and Recreation, Cohen and his colleagues at Columbia University taught TQM by helping the department undertake a set of two dozen quality improvement projects. Commissioner Betsy Gotbaum required each of her eight senior managers to propose and undertake three short-turnaround improvement projects. Columbia faculty trained the managers and eight senior aides (quality coordinators) to select, staff, and organize quality improvement teams. Employees began to learn TQM as they completed their initial twenty-four projects.

Finally, you need to go to training. If you are hesitant or not yet ready to bring TQM into your organization, attend a course with other managers, which will give you an orientation to the concepts, tools, and approaches used. If you are already convinced, you can schedule your training along with a group of other people from your own office. Once you learn the basics and believe in them, you can introduce all of your employees to the basic ideas and let your troops know that you will be moving toward a new style of work.

When he was at the EPA, Ronald Brand went to great lengths to be at the first full day of each three-day basic TQM training course offered to his employees. He did two important things there. In ten minutes he explained how he had arrived at the decision to implement TQM. In addition, Brand served as a cheerleader, interpreter, and translator. At that time, all the TQM courses were private-sector oriented. We found that among government employees there was almost a "knee-jerk" negative reaction to TQM examples based on industry practice. Sometimes it was as simple as the use of terms like *inventory* or *order backlog*. We had to help the group explore how these applied to their work. For example, were not sixty permit applications awaiting review a backlog? How did unpaid fines resemble accounts receivable? It was important to help people see how TQM concepts could apply to their work.

Scheduling Training

Once you as chief of your organization or an upper-level manager have been trained, you can train other parts of the organization in a variety of ways. Typically, we have seen a branch or division in a bureau or agency taking training as a group. Different trainers recommend groups of various sizes, ranging from 20 to 35. We know others who train in groups as large as 100, but we do not know what success they have had in implementation. It may be possible to train in larger groups if the trainees are going back to an organization that has built up a TQM culture already. However, we think that the main purpose of TQM training is orientation. The only way to really learn TQM is to gradually apply the core concepts in your daily work.

A variant on training people as an organizational unit is to train all participants involved in a single process, or group of processes. For example, you might train as a group all the regulators who request field samples, the field inspectors who gather or contract for the gathering of such samples, the laboratory staff who process or review the sampling data, and the budget office staffers who work on the finances related to sampling.

What this does is give them a running head start on implementation. Instead of using concocted generic examples to illustrate and learn about flow charts, fishbones, pareto charts, and customer diagnosis, employees immediately begin applying TQM to their own work. In fact, the group usually starts identifying problems and improvements during the training session, and before they leave training they can achieve agreement on process obstacles and improvements they want to tackle back at work. This gives a self-starting character to implementation, helping avoid the "waiting for the starting gun" behavior that we described at the beginning of this chapter. This training approach can also be accomplished within a single organizational unit by including a hands-on workshop as part of the course.

We also believe that it may be better to schedule the training over several weeks rather than conduct it in an intensive retreat atmosphere. The arguments made for the intensive approach to training are that (1) spending the evening together and being away from the workplace creates a team-building atmosphere; (2) it keeps people from letting daily work pressures interfere with the training sessions; (3) it is hard to get people to take time for this training even once, let alone for a series of sessions over a period of weeks; and (4) when you have to bring people in from a variety of widespread geographic locations for training, you can only do it one time. (This last argument has merit in some cases.)

We have been experimenting with an approach that calls for five four-hour sessions spread over a five-week period. We believe that this enables trainees to absorb and try out the things they have learned. We advocate some sort of group or individual homework assignment so that trainees have to apply lessons learned back at the job. For example, each trainee is asked to create a flow chart for his or her portion of a specific process, including the work of his or her supplier and customer. Problems, insights, and queries can then be discussed at the start of the next week's training session, which allows trainees to gain confidence in the use of the tools and begin making improvements in their work. More important, we believe five weeks of reinforcement created by a weekly four-hour training session and application on the job is likely to ease start-up problems and create a more enduring implementation program.

Obviously, this will be more feasible if you train your own people to be the trainers. They know the organization and its work and can schedule the half-day per week, which is much harder to do if you are using a contractor firm for the training: it may be too costly to pay for five trips, additional preparation time, and so on.

Schonberger, in *Building a Chain of Customers* (1982), tells about companies where workers have learned only one of the tools, such as the flow chart or pareto diagram, and by continuously applying that tool have made a series of ongoing improvements. The opposite of this is a three-day course that attempts to teach over twenty different tools, from force-field analysis to cost-benefit analysis.

Despite our particular preferences, we note that you, as a manager, need to make the decision about what type of TQM training will work best in your organization's culture, since there are no guarantees. On the other hand, we have seen organizations succeed whether they used the Deming, Juran, or Crosby approach and whether they were trained by group a, b, or c. Your personal leadership and the example you set will determine whether or not you succeed, regardless of the training you select. In fact, you may not have a choice in the training you use because your parent organization may have made that choice for you. For example, if you are one branch in a division, you may be required to participate and buy into the division training.

Knowing the Limits and Dangers of Advocacy

The best way to advocate TQM is to apply it yourself immediately. The day after you return from training, begin to make use of what you have learned. For example, you find yourself attending a meeting on a specific project. Raise questions in a "soft" manner, statements such as "I'm not sure who we think we are helping with this" (this is the "who is the customer" question) or "Are we clear on the process for getting this done? Can we sketch a flow chart of the process on the board to see if we are all talking about the same thing?" or "Why am I getting this work to review? Does ensuring quality really depend on my inspecting each piece of work at the end of the process? Can we change that?"

In a variety of ways you are beginning to get everyone to think about and use TQM concepts and tools. When people demonstrate this behavior, be sure to show your approval and congratulate them; this will reinforce the TQM behavior, since most people want to please the boss. It can be overdone, but it is a risk we would take. In the first few months of our OUST experience with TQM, a group met with Brand on a particular problem or program for an hour or more without using a single TQM tool to explain the problem or solution. Brand pointed this out and showed how they could have used TQM tools to their advantage for whatever it was they were trying to accomplish. Some months later at a TQM refresher for all employees, one OUST worker spoke up: "Ron, there are times when we solve the problem in another way, and then we do the charts after that." Brand responded, "Why would you do that? There are other ways to solve problems." The employee replied, "Because you kept pushing so hard on the use of charts. We felt we had to produce charts whether we needed them or not."

Needless to say, Brand adjusted his behavior after that. It is important to focus on the substance, not just the form, of TQM, but such excess by you as the leader of your organization is probably initially needed to get TQM genuinely ingrained. What is critical is establishing communication and feedback mechanisms that demonstrate your constancy of purpose. Organizations do not change automatically or overnight—they are organisms that must be nurtured, not machines to switch on and off. This means that advocates of organizational change must temper their arguments with realism and sensitivity. If constant improvement through work analysis and a customer orientation are to be truly embedded in your organization's culture you must allow time (even while providing daily stimulus and pressure) to adapt them to the specifics of your organization's goals, environment, and personnel.

Defending Use of TQM with Peers and Superiors

Many TQM authors and advocates argue that this new management system cannot be implemented without a firm commitment from the top. We do not agree. If you want to transform an organization of 15,000 people, you certainly do need the boss's commitment. However, if you are willing to transform your own unit of 5 or 10 people, then *you* are the top and all you need is to be sure of yourself. In the public sector, who is the top? The president? The governor? The agency chief? Or is it the division director, branch chief, or section chief? We are not saying that commitment from the top is not a good thing and a wonderful resource. We are saying that its absence is a poor excuse for not learning about and applying TQM to your work and better fulfilling your organization's purpose.

Implementing TQM in Spite of the Hierarchy

In every organization, no matter how low in the hierarchy, some piece of work is largely under its own control; otherwise, it is unlikely that you would see a separate organizational unit. These tasks may be the place to begin customer and work process analysis. In addition, every office performs a number of routine functions, ranging from answering the mail and phone to responding to legislative inquiries. These are also places where TQM can begin without approval from above.

One of the important things the boss can do is understand and participate in TQM enough to distinguish the genuine from the counterfeit. We have seen frequent occasions where people are asked what they are doing to implement TQM, or to report on their results (this, in itself, is the wrong thing to do). The response is often to sweep up any improvement or apparent improvement and package it as a TQM improvement. What is the harm in this? The troops know that it is counterfeit and they figure that it is the same old game. How can the boss help in these situations? To start, he or she can ask a few questions like: "How did you go about determining what the customers needed or wanted?" "What changes did you make in the process?" "How did you organize the team to improve the process and who was on it?" "What was the level of performance before you started the improvement work?" "How do you plan to determine how well the changes are working?"

In our view, TQM is a method of working. We believe it is so powerful and effective as a model that it can be infused into an organization from a variety of levels. It can be started at the individual level, which means that even if you do not manage other people's work you can analyze your own tasks. You can look for variation and attempt to develop new procedures for accomplishing your own work. You can analyze your day and attempt to increase the amount of time you devote to value-added work and reduce the time you spend on necessary but not value-added work. That is, you can spend more time on the work that directly results in a benefit to your customer and less on necessary organizational maintenance tasks, such as budget preparation. You can identify and communicate with your own customers and suppliers. No one needs to authorize you to work in this way, any more than you have been authorized to perform your tasks within the more traditional paradigm.

Further, we believe that this way of working is contagious because it produces better results. People who work this way get more done and accomplish more of what they set out to do. Most traditional managers allow you to carry out your work with some discretion. You need not label the steps of your tasks as customer analysis, analysis of current performance, work process analysis, and so on. TQM need not be seen as anything more than a different way of approaching work. As such, it can be done on some portion of any organization's tasks at any level in the organization all the way down to the individual.

Typical Attacks and Possible Responses

You should expect to be attacked by people who are resistant to change and feel threatened by a TQM initiative. TQM will be attacked as

- A fad—the latest of a series of useless management innovations from ZBB to quality circles
- Only useful to private-sector manufacturing firms
- Symbolic, superficial, and not applicable to real work
- A waste of time in an action-packed, pressure-cooker public-sector environment

We have found that when defending TQM it is best to strip it down to its essential concepts. Each author or TQM guru, and certainly each TQM consulting firm, tries to sell a complete integrated package of ideas and practices. Many of the rules and guidelines presented by the TQM merchants are useful, but each organization will need to develop its own blend of practices. People from organizations that have successfully practiced TQM for more than a couple of years all say that you should not copy the specifics of their organizations' program since, after about a year, any organization will have shaped its program to fit its own culture. Some of the lessons that we have learned in our governmental experience may not be appropriate to your agency, for example.

As mentioned earlier, TQM can be reduced to several basic concepts: (1) an emphasis on quality as defined by your customers, (2) continuous staff analysis of their own tasks to improve performance, and (3) working with suppliers so that you start with high-quality supplies. Few people will argue against the idea of paying attention to the public and their needs and constantly improving the standard operating procedures that structure the performance of tasks. What is the argument against these ideas? "Ignore the public and allow SOPs to deteriorate." The usual arguments are not this silly, but a frequently unstated feeling exists that reexamining SOPs is not worth the trouble.

Using Results and Examples

The best argument for TQM is the results that it generates. Data on savings in production processes are produced as part of the process of analyzing and improving performance. It is relatively easy to demonstrate that a TQM work analysis results in lower costs and compressed schedules. For example, let us say that you have eliminated a report because you have decided through a TQM process that it is not value-added or necessary work. You will not have a hard time quantifying the workhours or days saved and translating that into a dollar figure. To convey the importance of constantly eliminating all waste, one of our favorite approaches in working with a group goes as follows: the group identifies a small step in a process that they agree is a waste but "it only takes five minutes." We ask how many times a day that step has to be performed. "Ten times a day," is the answer. We then ask them to multiply that by 260 workdays (50 minutes × 260 = 13,000 minutes) and to divide the result (13,000 minutes) by 60 to get the hours: 216. The 216 hours translates into 5.4 workweeks. We then point out that they are wasting that number of weeks each year on this unnecessary little step. Is it worth doing the work to change it, we ask? The answer is usually yes.

Whenever possible we urge you to avoid calling attention to your TQM efforts outside your organizational unit or section until you have results to demonstrate success. Arguments about the logic and attractiveness of TQM concepts are far less persuasive than actual results.

Teaching and Consulting with Colleagues in Response to Requests

Many managers are frustrated with their inability to accomplish what they set out to achieve. Even before they understand TQM, they are frequently impressed by the energy it unleashes and the confidence that it gives employees. One result is that you may find yourself called on by colleagues in another unit of your organization to help them get started on TQM. This can be time-consuming, but it can help spread the ideas throughout the organization and build internal political support for this new way of working.

Although it is possible to start TQM in isolation, ultimately agencywide procedures such as management by objectives and bean-counting management information systems should be altered in order to fully implement TQM. To do this you will need allies. Do not limit your help to those above you in the organizational hierarchy. Within the constraints of getting your own job done, try as hard as you can to help colleagues who seem serious about adopting TQM.

Developing a Supportive Organizational Culture and Incentive System

A critical and difficult task for a manager attempting to implement TQM is to alter the incentive structure to reward improvements. It is important to provide a reward even if the payoff will occur months or years later. Typically, we reward those who respond to emergencies and not those who build and maintain or improve systems that reduce or eliminate emergencies. An illustration that we are all familiar with is the situation where a group is rewarded because its members worked so hard, including weekends and nights, to complete their work over a period of months. The reaction from other groups in the same organization is that if they had planned and done their work right the first time they would not have had to work so hard. They view it as "inefficiency rewarded," which has a negative impact on morale.

It is also important to foster and use employee suggestions, to encourage frequent experimentation to improve work processes. Successful experiments are not the only ones that should be rewarded; reward experiments that fail, if they provide important insights about work processes. Finally, find ways to reward group effort, especially since most personnel evaluation systems emphasize individual accomplishment.

The key to rearranging the incentive system is to fully adopt the new paradigm about work and management. The people reporting directly to you should be rewarded for their effort to implement TQM. We recognize that providing material rewards to top performers and successful work teams is sometimes difficult in government. However, even public organizations have a variety of resources to deploy as incentives: choice assignments, better office space, public recognition, or even simple expressions of gratitude. Rewards like these, along with promotions and raises, are all opportunities to applaud improved performance, high-quality work analysis, and successful customer-driven projects. Effective rewards we have seen or used that are available to most managers include·

- Implementing small improvements quickly
- Starting each staff, monthly, or quarterly meeting with quality and work improvement as the first items on the agenda
- Asking questions about and sincerely congratulating people on quality projects that are in process or have been completed
- Going to a team's workspace to be briefed on work in progress

- Taking a team to a meeting with senior managers to present their work
- Allowing the group to present its work to other groups in other organizations upon request, supplying travel funds if needed
- Asking about and congratulating supervisors who have quality projects or work in their units (sometimes we have seen this drive the supervisor to find out more about what he or she is being congratulated on)
- Leading the applause when a team demonstrates a worthwhile TQM effort or result

In other words, attention from the manager is one of the most important components of a successful TQM program. Organizations that have been working with TQM for more than a year or two emphasize that, once you consistently reward TQM-oriented behavior, quality improvement will begin to become embedded in your organization's culture. People will learn that questioning SOPs is not only acceptable but necessary if they want to succeed. After a while, it will become part of the "lore" of the organization and will be transmitted to new employees when they are hired.

The specific behaviors you will reward include worker honesty and amnesty, work analysis, prevention of mistakes and waste, customer and supplier communication, and continuous improvement. This means that you will need to learn not to shoot the messenger who brings you bad news and, in fact, to reward the person brave enough to be honest about the situation. This takes courage, because someone is demonstrating that you have been wrong about something, and there is a natural human tendency to be defensive and to punish such truth-tellers. Early on, however, pick a visible example of someone who has discovered flaws in something you have invented and make a big deal about rewarding that person.

Techniques for Making Improvement Continuous

Once you have invested considerable energy in bringing TQM into your organization, the next challenge is to maintain an atmosphere that is conducive to continuous improvement, building the expectation that small, steady improvement is a way of organizational life. Employees should learn that TQM work analysis and customer contact is no longer the exception; it is the way the organization works. We do not depend on achieving one big magical production breakthrough but learn to understand and communicate the power of hundreds of small, creative incremental improvements that will cumulatively achieve significant change. Constant reinforcement is essential.

Just as important as these measures are the signals you send by your daily actions. One way to show the importance of quality efforts is by not allowing an interruption if you or others are engaged in quality activities. Push your managers on this. The time for you to hear a report from a quality team is at least as significant as the other activities for which you do not allow interruptions.

The same is true for training. One middle manager recently described her two days of quality training, which her boss had ordered all supervisors to attend. The boss came in late, left early, and openly worked on a stack of in-box work while the training was going on. She and the rest of the staff were furious and disheartened. The boss destroyed any hope they had that he was serious about quality and improvement, but they knew he would now report to his superiors that he and all his managers were "trained." He would "get his quality training card punched" and that would be the end of it. A helpful method is to use the "100 Mile Rule" in these situations. This asks you to behave as if your office is 100 miles from where the meeting or training is occurring. If so, would you respond to a specific interruption or emergency by leaving and flying or driving back to the office? If not, then you should not be permitting the interruption to interfere with your meeting or training (Scholtes and others, 1988).

Another way to show that you are serious about quality efforts is to be sure that teams have the tools they need, for example, a place to meet, a flip chart or blackboard, special pens, Post-Its, and so on. We have seen teams have to cancel meetings because they were bumped from the room they were to meet in. The boss usually has an office big enough for a team to meet. Offer your office as a meeting place when no other is available, even if you are not going to be part of the meeting. You can always use the desk of someone who is attending the meeting.

A third way to show support is by purchasing books or renting videos on quality. How often have you seen a team of workers excited about some new area and wanting to learn more so that they can move forward? The system says to order one book through the agency library and wait weeks or months for it. We used small-purchase authority to buy several books in one day. You need to recognize that this is an investment, not a cost. One team achieving improvements in their work will return the $25 or $75 investment one hundred or one thousand times over, but your authorization of fast action will send your employees an even stronger signal.

Top Management Commitment to TQM

Top management commitment is a luxury. If you have it, fine, but the probability that the top manager of your organization will have such a commitment is low. What do we mean by a committed top management? These top officers have been trained in TQM; in the normal course of working they ask questions about who the customer is and what process the organization is trying to change or improve; they aggressively foster and support continuous improvement efforts.

Committed top managers will be thinking about quality when they address every issue. For example, two regulators meet with a top manager to discuss a legal issue. Should the wording in a regulation be "should" or "shall"? The quality manager will ask who the customer is for this regulation and change. Is it the state legislator, a local permit writer, or a factory supervisor? Where in the process of whatever they are to do is the change (an improvement, it is hoped) supposed to take place? By what process do they hope to see these changed words (should or shall) actually put into practice? How will they know if it does or does not take place in the "real world"? These questions will help clarify, settle, or eliminate the disputed issue.

Is top management commitment really needed, however? The SMED workshop discussed in Chapter Two provides an example of successful TQM implementation that occurred without top management support. At that workshop, Brand heard workers in printing plants, auto equipment companies, bakeries, cheese factories, casket factories, and publishing tell their stories. They were achieving changeovers that formerly took twelve to thirty hours in less than ten minutes. Repeatedly, they pointed out that engineering departments and/or top management were not involved in these success stories.

You Can Implement TQM Through Your Own Actions

We need not wait for the comprehensive, total commitment of top management as a precondition of getting started. Get started yourself. Have you gone beyond orientation in your TQM learning? Are you constantly learning about and asking the customer questions? Are you looking at *your* processes and continuously trying to improve them?

The following checklist summarizes some key management behaviors needed to implement TQM.

1. Visibly attend and participate in the full TQM orientation training course that you use, so that you know what has been taught and can understand and use the TQM language with others.
2. When problems arise or when new programs/services are designed, focus on enabling managers and workers to do the job right the first time. Your questions should be about the process, helping to define who the customer is and what data are needed to measure quality and productivity performance and improvements.
3. Know whether you and your employees share a common set of beliefs and if you are effectively communicating your priorities. If employees are unclear about your priorities,

the results are poor day-to-day decisions and frustration for them and you.

4. Try not to solve problems exclusively from your perspective. Actively seek middle-management and worker input to key decisions.
5. In your normal contacts, let people know that you are interested in their quality improvement projects. What are they working on? What are they finding? When is the next team meeting? Ask if you can sit in (unobtrusively). If there is a way you can help—such as checking with a major customer—ask if they would like you to do that.
6. Enable your people to do a better job, with fewer emergencies and rework, by meeting personally with your major customers and suppliers.
7. In the normal course of managing, ask questions such as "What is the process here and what is going wrong?" "Who do we consider to be the customers here and in what priority order?" "How should we measure quality on this step, process, or problem? Do we have a way to do it? Can we start? When?"

Recruiting Managers to TQM

Organizational change of any type can be a difficult, emotionally wrenching process (see Chapter Four). The people who work for you have often made a considerable intellectual, professional, social, and emotional investment in the current way of doing work. Your best people have often made the deepest commitment to the existing organizational order. Senior people may simply lump TQM into the grab bag of management fads they have weathered during their years in public service: PPBS (planning, programming, and budgeting systems), MIS (management information systems), MBO (management by objectives), PERT (program evaluation and review technique), OD (organizational development), and ZBB (zero-based budgeting), to name some of the more popular ones. Each of these techniques has been oversold as a new management technology, each has had some utility, but none has delivered as promised. Here comes TQM, once again promising to revolutionize management. Senior people and students of public management have every reason to be skeptical.

Moreover, the almost religious fervor we have seen demonstrated by followers of Deming and other quality gurus contributes to suspicion of TQM. It may very well be that the key to excellence in public management is simply a deep commitment to such excellence. The effective public manager searches for tools that fit the current culture and popular mindset and uses them to help transform an organization. TQM is probably best seen in that context.

The worldwide movement for democracy, self-expression, and human rights is in many respects a demand for human dignity and a measure of self-determination in an increasingly complex, crowded, and mechanized world. Workplace democracy and cooperatives may be unworkable given our tradition of hierarchy and the need for single points of control in complex organizations. Something between strict hierarchy and worker control is needed. TQM provides workers with a significant voice in the design of work but leaves decision making in the hands of management. It is probably this mix of participation and authority that makes TQM appropriate at this particular point in time.

We believe that when recruiting your management to TQM you must avoid overselling it. The three core concepts are presented in Chapter Three:

1. Working with suppliers to ensure that the supplies you utilize in your work processes are designed for your use
2. Employee analysis of work processes in order to improve their functioning and reduce process variation
3. Close communication with customers to identify and understand what they want and how they define quality

When introducing these ideas to your middle management, it is important to be specific and use examples from your own organization to explain TQM concepts, although you may send your key people to a TQM training session to introduce them to the subject matter. You may find it useful to talk about problems you have had with poor supplies or contractors. Sketch out some scenarios to illustrate how closer communication with suppliers might have resulted in a better quality program. Do the same thing when discussing your own work processes and communication with your customers. Illustrate the benefits of paying more attention to suppliers, customers, and work processes by doing a postmortem examination of something that recently went wrong in your organization.

In addition to describing the advantages of TQM, it is critical to discuss the risks as well. There is a transition period, which varies from organization to organization, where the costs of TQM may outweigh the benefits, at least in the short run. Initially, employees must be trained to understand a new way of working and be weaned from a variety of outmoded work habits, and this process may result in a temporary reduction in productivity. Many government agencies operate under constant pressure and do not believe that they can take the time to go through training, analyze their own work, or interact with suppliers and customers. During this transition period, it may appear to your colleagues that you are diverting time and money from the organization's regular work.

You may also find that your work analysis identifies some agencywide standard operating procedures that ought to be dropped. Sometimes you will find it worthwhile to seek an exemption from these SOPs, presenting arguments that can entail risks to your organization and sometimes to your own career. More frequently, you will avoid a direct confrontation and seek to find a shortcut that will enable you to comply with the SOP but with a lower expenditure of organizational resources. For example, in meeting an agencywide requirement, OUST was able to reduce the material to be prepared and reviewed from over twenty-five pages to four. This saved significant time for the tank program's regional and state agency customers. It also encouraged our managers by showing that radical improvements could be made by genuinely determining and meeting customer needs.

The risks of adopting TQM in government can be substantially reduced by the manner in which it is introduced into an organization. When presenting TQM to middle managers or workers, it is important to stress that there will be a gradual transition period. Inevitably, parts of your work will be performed without work analysis and without discussions with suppliers and customers. Although you will be able to score some quick victories with early quality improvement projects, some problems will undoubtedly require a longer effort before they result in improvement. The key to introducing TQM is to recognize that it is a long-term and never-ending process that requires consistent effort and patience.

One danger of moving too quickly is that you may not really have brought your employees along. They will give you the form of TQM analysis without the substance; you will be swimming in flow charts and fishbone diagrams, but your organization's work processes may remain unchanged. Do not expect instant change, or overnight success.

We are convinced that managers who learn to work this way will be sought after professionally. TQM-oriented managers are able to present a coherent view of management to those they work for and those who work for them. They are results oriented but conscious of the need to elicit staff participation in designing work processes. The evidence we have seen in the federal government indicates that TQM can enhance a manager's reputation and ability to accomplish goals. Clearly, this is an argument that should be used in introducing TQM to management.

Gauging Acceptance and Confronting Resistance

Some managers will be slow in learning TQM or may just remain unconvinced of its usefulness. Others may be quite excited about the concepts but unable to translate them into their everyday work. Another group will talk about TQM as extra work to be done in addition to their regular work. Early on, your employees will need to teach each other to approach all work through TQM, but often it will be easy to lapse into old ways of working.

All organizations are built on collections of standard

operating procedures (SOPs), predesignated organizational routines established to respond to specific, clearly defined environmental and internal stimuli. Bureaucratic organizations can be seen as collections of coordinated standard operating procedures. Organizations require SOPs because it is impossible to rationally analyze every issue that they face. Organizations look for shortcuts that allow them to react to a given specific stimulus with a patterned, virtually automatic set of responses. One fact of organizational life is that SOPs are quite stable and long lasting. TQM's overarching goal is to constantly analyze and modify them to make them more effective and efficient. The normal tendency of most organizations is to look for satisfactory SOPs and, once that point is reached, move to other issues.

People develop a comfort level around routines and a fair amount of ease and expertise in implementing them. Some of the resistance to TQM stems from a fundamental opposition to changing practices that seem to work. If it is not broken, why fix it? Of course, even a TQM organization will only gradually modify routines, and it does so with the active participation of those who carry them out. SOPs make it possible to simplify organizational responses to complex and frequently unstable environments. You will not have the time to assess every SOP in your organization; therefore, some of the work will inevitably continue as in the past.

One method for determining whether or not your organization is resisting TQM is to identify the work processes or SOPs that have been changed. If you have been attempting to implement TQM in your organization for six months and cannot find at least a few significant changes in work processes, you are definitely facing resistance.

Recruiting Employees to TQM

The nature of the authority relationship between management and employees changes under TQM. Management must still retain responsibility for fundamental decisions, but those decisions are frequently shaped by information collected by employees who are engaged in work analysis. Employees and first-line supervisors are no longer expected to simply carry out SOPs designed by management. They are now expected and encouraged to think about those work processes, an expectation created by the TQM training they have been given, the scheduling of time to meet to improve processes, and management asking for their views on a process.

Here is a recent example from our experience. Management had planned a construction job to be completed in fifteen days. In an effort to find ways to get the job done even faster, they called in the foremen responsible for getting the job done. In reviewing the proposed plan, the foremen forcefully pointed out that the time allocated for laying the concrete was inadequate. It was midsummer with temperatures in the high 90s, which made the tools overheat and work much tougher and increased worker fatigue. Therefore, they would not be able to lay the standard amount of concrete in the normal ten-hour day. These same foremen and their crew members, however, found additional ways to reduce the time needed for completion of the job. Management listened and factored this information into a new schedule. This interaction between workers and management changed management decisions and altered traditional decision processes.

Managers and employees must have a clear idea of the needs of the user or customer related to the work they perform. Employees cannot obtain information about customer preferences if they do not communicate with customers, which will affect the monopoly of information on customer preferences that is often held by management in some organizations. This changes the nature of the power relationship between management and employees. An example of this occurred in an office that had to prepare a weekly report to the agency head. The usual routine was to do the report, get it revised and reworked at three levels, and rush it out in a week, with no feedback to the people preparing the report in the originating office. Led by one midlevel manager who had taken her TQM training to heart, the staff asked the customer to tell them how he used the report. Armed with this information, employees were able to be more directly responsive and reduce the amount of time it took to complete the report. This seems like an obvious and insignificant example; after speaking to the customer, the staff cut two hours of work off each weekly report, which meant that two and one-half workweeks a year had been wasted because the workers had not been allowed to speak to the customer to find out what he needed.

It is important that managers give workers the time to talk directly to suppliers and customers. When the customer is a senior manager to whom workers cannot get access, the manager will need to communicate for the workers. Direct communication with customers is better, if it is feasible.

This also applies to benchmarking, which involves going to other organizations that do similar work and are highly regarded to learn if you can adapt or make use of some of their methods to improve your work processes. These visits are a worthwhile activity for workers and managers. Do not limit these interactions to managers only, however, since doing so would not enable you to find out what it really takes to make the improved methods work. It is best to have workers talking to workers. Clearly, working this way permits the worker's expertise to give him or her a more important role in the agency's work and decisions.

The most important point to emphasize when selling TQM to employees is that it is a technique that can enhance an organization's well-being. Although management and employee roles will change, both will benefit. Employees gain influence over work processes, and management improves its ability to achieve an organization's goals.

Establishing the Credibility of the New Management System

The key to building the credibility of TQM with employees is to demonstrate that it can work. Initially, employees may not trust management's offer of amnesty. One way to overcome mistrust is to reward employees for participating in work analyses. Make a big deal out of your organization's first quality improvement projects. Take visible, concrete steps to implement the first work process improvements identified by employees. Provide time and resources to interact with customers and suppliers. Take part in quality improvement projects yourself, no matter how senior you are. Make an effort to quantify the savings you are generating from the improved work processes and outputs you are developing.

It is particularly important that employees see you give up some of your own favorite practices and perquisites in response to TQM analyses. Monitor your own middle managers to ensure that they are rewarding rather than punishing employees who develop work improvements. We have seen many examples of managers who encourage TQM work analysis and then stifle the suggestions that employees develop.

Let us face it, many people are insecure and can easily feel threatened. An aggressive employee who comes up with suggested work improvements may be seen as a threat to an insecure manager. After all, the work process being changed is one designed by, or at least accepted by, this insecure manager. Managers must have a certain amount of courage to admit that the old way, which was "their way," is wrong. Humor is a big help here, both in work group presentations and in showing that the manager recognizes that he or she is sometimes a primary obstacle.

Do not underestimate how difficult it may be to convince your employees and other managers to develop a new way of working. You are attempting to bring about a fundamental change in the way they think about work. Why should we expect instant acceptance for such a major step? Bringing TQM into an organization is a long and difficult process. It is useful to think of it as a campaign with discrete and critical phases, one of which is the conscious set of steps taken to enhance the credibility of the new system. Each organization must develop its own approach to establishing and reinforcing the key concepts of quality improvement:

- Focusing on improvement instead of specific numerical targets and goals
- Encouraging suggestions from everyone involved in the work process and obtaining those suggestions through the use of TQM

- Experimenting constantly with new work processes and with standard operating procedures

Expect resistance and challenges to the new system early in the change process. It is important that you have fully absorbed the central concepts of TQM and believe that you can consistently apply them (or your own version). If you are not fully convinced of the usefulness of Deming's version of TQM, or our approach, develop your own version. If the system is not credible to you, it will not be credible to your employees.

Typical Problems in Recruiting Employees and Responses to Those Problems

In any organization there will be people who embrace change and enjoy it and those that resist change and hate it. Beyond the employee attitude toward change itself, you will encounter a variety of reactions based on the individual's work experiences and understanding of the core concepts of TQM.

Many government organizations see themselves as under constant external pressure to perform, and employees in those organizations tend to feel overworked, believing that they are too busy to spend time creating a flow chart of their own work or determining their customers' needs. They feel they cannot find the time to be trained in the basics of TQM, and if they are managers, they are unwilling to allow their employees to participate. The idea of stopping, even for a few minutes, to examine their own operation is alien and unacceptable.

For these "staff-in-a-hurry," a variety of approaches are possible. One is to ask them to stay after work, or participate in training during their time off. A second is to demonstrate that the time devoted to TQM training and work analysis is an investment. If you can provide evidence that TQM can save time and help relieve pressure, you may convince this type of person to give it a try. One key strategy here is to suggest working on a particular process that bothers them and has good potential for short-term improvement.

A second type of problem is the employee who rejects the idea that a government official can prioritize customers. This person argues that government must serve all of the people, so focusing on and learning about the preferences of any specific set of customers is unfair and even unethical. Related are those employees who believe that they know better than the public what the public needs. In an environmental agency, we have heard the argument that if the people prefer employment in a dirty factory to a healthy environment, their preference is not valid. We have heard similar arguments made by social workers when discussing their welfare clients.

Customer analysis is difficult in the public sector, but it does not mean that a government official should twist the law and simply "give people what they want." Obviously there are boundaries on what is feasible to deliver to a customer, just as in the private sector customers might prefer a five-cent hamburger, but there is no way to deliver such a product. People who provide services must define the boundaries of what is feasible and identify preferences from within those boundaries. In operational terms this means that whenever practical, and as often as possible, substitute your customer's judgment of quality for your own. We are too willing, most of the time, to rely on our "expertise" and superior knowledge of the situation, rather than checking customer preferences.

The appropriate response to the employee who rejects the feasibility of customer analysis and communication is to demonstrate how it can help that particular person's work. Once you can establish this feasibility, you will need to show how customer preferences can be incorporated into the design of a program, eliminating unnecessary work and reducing customer complaints.

Another common problem is that employees sometimes have difficulty seeing their work as part of a production process. At the heart of work analysis is a conceptual framework that places the worker in a specific relationship with work. Figure 6.1 is a graphic illustration of the work process. Work is the process of taking a supply and performing some type of operation on that supply that adds value to it. As Figure 6.1 indicates, the arbitrator, under TQM, of the quality of the product received is the customer. This fairly straightforward description of the

Figure 6.1. Illustration of the Work Process.

Seeing Work as Part of a Process

Supplier	Supply	Production	Product/Service	Customer
From whom do I get my work?	In what form do I get it?	What do I do with it? (Inspect it, or add value?)	What do I send on to the next step?	Who gets my completed work?

work process is not the typical way that people see work and their relationship to it. Sometimes professionals resist seeing themselves as an element in a production process. In addition to the problems people see in working with customers, employees also identify difficulties in working with suppliers.

One frequently cited issue is that in most governmental settings it is not possible to develop close, long-term relationships with external suppliers, due to rules governing competitive bidding. There are several responses to that particular issue. The first is that competitive bidding does not preclude multiyear, even fairly long-term contracts. Once the bidding process is complete, government employees are free to interact with contractors and a close, interactive relationship can be established with contractors and suppliers.

Many government contracts include performance-based bonuses, and contractors are often left guessing as to what type of performances will win these bonuses. Employees should be encouraged to work closely with these suppliers, to allocate time to working with the contractor to develop product specifications and expectations, not simply drop a work order in the mail. Employees who manage contractors sometimes enjoy the sense of control they have in a work world that is frequently characterized by lack of control, and they are reluctant to give up their right to order contractors around. The appropriate response to this problem is first to create an environment where employees participate in the design of their own work and therefore increase their sense of control over that work, and second to convince them that they will enjoy their relationship with their contractor and produce more from the relationship if they learn to work together.

Another potential response to the issue of supplier relationships is to note that many of your suppliers are not contractors. People within your organization, interest groups, scholars, and a variety of other organizations provide your employees with supplies in the form of data, reports, opinions, and cases. Your personnel office supplies a formal hiring process. An interest group may provide you with the data that you use in a report. Your field office provides you with an analysis of a critical operational issue. Your employees will generally benefit from a close relationship with these suppliers in order to facilitate a clearer understanding of your organization's needs. Again, the best way to convince a reluctant employee of the usefulness of this established close contact is to provide examples of ways in which such a relationship has improved some output.

Developing a Core Group Interested in Organizational Change

It is not possible to predict which parts of your organization will embrace or resist TQM. Some of your most senior people may never become convinced of its merit, and some fairly junior people may end up being very important change agents. Our experience has been that where change produces improved results it becomes contagious. You need to identify people in your organization who are most receptive to TQM, as demonstrated by their daily behavior, and then pay extra attention to nurturing their improvement projects and their learning.

The critical point that we are making in this chapter is that organizational change is a difficult, long-term process. People benefit by and are attached to the way they approach work. To change something as fundamental as how your organization approaches work, expect that you will need to devote a great deal of attention to stimulating, nurturing, and reinforcing change.

The next chapter provides a case study of how a partial changeover to TQM was brought about in one governmental organization. We do not present this case as a model but, rather, we include it to chart the evolution of TQM in one organizational setting. We hope that you will see some things that look familiar and can be of help. One of the purposes of this book is to delineate the lessons we learned from that experience. We hope that the case is instructive and that you will avoid making some of the mistakes described in Chapter Seven.

PART THREE

Total Quality Management
in
the Real World

CHAPTER 7

Bringing TQM to the
Environmental Protection Agency's
Office of Underground Storage Tanks

How did TQM get started at the OUST office? Why did OUST get started? Looking back, what could have been changed or improved?

First Steps in the Search for Management Innovation

The federal program to regulate leaking underground storage tanks was new when Ronald Brand joined it in August 1985. The Office of Underground Storage Tanks (OUST) was officially established in January 1986. In its first three years OUST focused most of its attention on developing underground storage tank regulations. However, OUST established a small implementation unit at the start, so the organization's members would always be thinking of the practical realities of doing the work covered by, or stemming from, the regulations.

In doing this work, Brand and his senior managers used management tools and experience gathered over the years. These included PERT (program evaluation and review) charts to establish timetables, communication efforts to provide clear guidance to tank owners, and simplified requirements and forms. The OUST management team took a number of innovative approaches to the program. It felt good about these and was recognized for them by others in the EPA, the states, and the regulated community.

Searching for Private-Sector Metaphors:
The Franchise Approach

As management thought about the organization's relationship with state governments, they searched for an innovative model to govern OUST's main interorganizational relationships. The management team wanted to avoid the highly centralized "look-over-the-shoulder" approach that is typical of many federal-state relationships. The model selected by Brand and his senior managers was the franchise, which permits central control of standards and allows for a great deal of local discretion over how programs are implemented. Brand brought in franchisers such as McDonald's, Seven-Eleven Stores, Century 21 realtors, and Servicemaster to tell how they established services at thousands of locations, maintained the level of service at these varied locations, and constantly improved services. The two main principles they taught were: (1) There are no cash registers at headquarters—all results occur in the field. (2) Therefore, your principal job is to assist and support the field. OUST incorporated these concepts and took a number of actions that distinguished the program from traditional programs—especially in its dealings with the states, who were the franchisees.

But Brand, as director of the tank office, remembers his concern when the private-sector franchisers asked, "When you go out to your franchisees (the states), what do you bring to the table?" They asked this question against a background of their experience in which field audits were conducted by people who had years of experience in line and store operations. This meant that their field representatives could identify and anticipate problems and, moreover, had credibility when offering suggestions or pushing for better performance. However, senior managers in the EPA headquarters and the EPA's ten regional offices did not often possess such direct, practical line experience. So when they asked, "What do you bring to the table?" OUST managers made such replies as "grant money, knowledge of our regulations, and knowledge of financial reporting requirements under our statute."

These experienced private-sector franchisers had trouble accepting these as a substitute for experienced practical help with the specific operating problems that the state agency personnel were facing. They intuitively recognized that OUST was required to distribute the grant dollars since Congress expected the EPA to spend the allocated money. They sensed that much of OUST's interpretative role on the regulations and reporting requirements was because the regulations and reporting requirements were overly complex and poorly written.

This point made a deep impression on the members of the OUST organization. Others did not seem worried by it; after all, most of the rest of the EPA's programs operated in the same top-down way with few people who had practical experience. Federal agencies frequently operate as if the federal-state relationship is a parent-child relationship. The idea is that agencies decide when state organizations are old enough to cross the street by themselves or to go off on their own. The federal government continuously disregards the fact that states have run programs in many areas of government on their own and without the federal government's "great wisdom."

Discovering TQM

Then Brand happened to come across Mary Walton's book *The Deming Management Method.* One reading convinced him that this was what he had been looking for as a way to make a genuine difference, and he then read every TQM book he could find, including Deming's *Quality, Productivity, and Competitive Position* and *Out of the Crisis,* Philip Crosby's *Quality Is Free,* Joseph Juran's *Juran on Planning for Quality,* and Kaoru Ishikawa's *Guide to Quality Control.* One idea that helped Brand in these early learning ventures was that he had always looked at any operation that involved hundreds or thousands of transactions, interactions, postings, or transfers as a type of assembly line. Therefore, he found it relatively easy to mentally adapt things from a factory or industry setting to "softer" government administrative and program functions or nonprofit operations such as hospitals or clinics.

As we have talked with employees and managers throughout the public sector, we have discovered that many find it difficult to adapt innovative private-sector or manufacturing practices to public-sector service organizations. Similarly, we have found that private-sector managers are equally resistant to learning from the public sector's great skill at operating in a fishbowl and thriving under conditions of great fluidity and ambiguity. As a professor to future public managers, Cohen often tells students of the importance of the habit of lifelong learning. The ability to search for new ideas and be open to constant learning separates excellent from mediocre managers. In fact, in *Thriving on Chaos*, Tom Peters argues that the effective manager must learn to love change and be able to thrive in ambiguous situations.

Because of Brand's background in management and his consistent emphasis on simplicity and reducing red tape, the ideas he began incorporating into his daily work did not seem strange to his colleagues. He also had the advantage of being able to pick his employees for the newly formed office, so he hired a number of like-minded managers and workers who kept creating better and simpler ways to do things—on their own.

Initially Brand could not get his employees to see why he thought that process flow charts on the real work done in the field were important. Finally, Brand asked a consultant, not experienced in tank work, to prepare a flow chart of the steps involved in closing and/or removing a gasoline underground storage tank. When unfurled and tacked to the wall in Brand's office, it extended over four feet and included ninety-seven steps. When OUST's middle managers saw the chart, they were upset and dubious. "Why was it done?" "How will we use it?" "We can't be bothered with all that detail." "How do you know it's complete or correct?" All these questions were skeptical and showed that clearly the managers considered this a waste of time and money.

Educating Everyone About TQM

Despite this apathetic or confused reaction, Brand purchased twenty copies of Mary Walton's book and gave them to all of the EPA's underground tank program regional and headquarters managers. A few became interested and started to lobby for TQM training, so after six months of reading, learning, and testing Brand decided that OUST had to adopt TQM. He contacted Conway Quality in Nashua, New Hampshire, because he had read about them in Mary Walton's book and attended a seminar that Conway conducted at the University of Tennessee. Bill Conway was the primary instructor that day and impressively communicated his grounding in the basic philosophy of TQM. This seminar was followed by a trip to the company's offices in New Hampshire where Brand spent four hours talking with Jim Copley, vice president of Conway Quality, as well as Ellen Kendall, an experienced trainer and practitioner of TQM. We have found that demonstrated experience in doing TQM is essential if the trainer is to have credibility. The first issue we raise with TQM trainers or consultants seeking to sell us their services is to ask them to demonstrate how TQM is used in their own operation and to give specific examples of work with other clients. The Conway team's experience showed in both their presentation and in their responses to questions or suggestions, and Brand decided to hire them to provide TQM training for OUST.

Training the Entire Organization

Over the next five months, OUST completed five two-and-a-half-day TQM workshops. Each one included about thirty staff. Training sessions included headquarters and field, clerical, and technical and management personnel, and even two or three state program directors. OUST held the sessions at different locations around the country to accommodate the field people.

Brand attended all three days of the first and last workshops. In the other sessions he attended the first day. At each session Brand opened with a ten-minute explanation of why OUST needed TQM. He emphasized that one thing was definite: this was the way the organization was going to operate and manage—that was not a choice. Brand had decided that he would use TQM to transform his organization, and he was not willing to revisit that decision. But from that point on, within a TQM approach, employees would be making the choices on how to improve their operations. Since TQM is primarily a way of thinking about the customer and work processes, the decision to work in a TQM way left considerable discretion to employees in shaping the organization's program and direction. Brand had concluded that he wanted a customer-driven, constantly improving program and that TQM gave him the management paradigm and tools he needed to make that happen.

As the classes progressed, some individuals from other operations such as budget, contracts, grants, and policy analysis joined the training. A few of the EPA's upper-level managers became curious and asked to attend, and of course, OUST gladly "made room" for them. We mention this sequence in partial response to the TQM dogma that you cannot begin TQM without "commitment from the top." In government, however, the "top" is often difficult to identify. Ronald Brand was the national program manager for the underground tank program, so in this sense he might be seen as the top. However, he reported to an assistant administrator who reported to an administrator who ultimately reported to the president. Brand was not at the top of this hierarchy, but he was high enough and had enough discretion to experiment with TQM.

When Brand started TQM training in OUST, he had a lot of trouble finding quality trainers who were experienced about TQM in government. This situation has changed in the past five years, but at that time the trainers' experience was primarily in industry and some work with the military. Most of the experience was in manufacturing rather than administration, and as a result, they used private-sector examples throughout the training. Many of the trainees complained and said they wanted more government examples. One of Brand's key roles in the training was to help others relate the business examples to their government work.

We observed that about one-third of each class responded enthusiastically, one-third said, "Go away and don't bother me with this TQM stuff," and one-third said, "Let's wait and see how this works out and whether it will last." One immediate payoff from the training was that the entire organization adopted a common vocabulary. Phrases such as "value-added work," "rework," "necessary but not value-added work," and "amnesty" were quickly put into use. Surprisingly, the themes and vocabulary seemed to play into underlying values that were already there. Remember that much of the work focused on implementation and practicality, and the vocabulary seemed to give us all a shorthand way of expressing TQM's underlying values. The training also seemed to encourage us to remember that the current way of doing business was not unchangeable.

Applying the TQM Training

As each group finished the training, they began to do small individual quality improvement projects. Three or four people got together because they felt frustrated by a certain process and decided to try to improve it. People volunteered for the teams, which rarely numbered more than three or four people. Teams tackled problems such as quicker response from headquarters on requests from OUST regional program coordinators, attempting to improve OUST's accountability and reporting system, improving transmittal of telephone messages, immediate response on telephone inquiries from the public, and making scarce personal computers more available for use by all employees. One branch put up a board listing the employees and placed a silver decal alongside their names as they came up with improvement ideas. Brand proudly went in one day to offer an idea, only to find out that someone else had already thought of it, so he had to wait to receive his first silver decal. With a new group being trained each month, these freshly trained troops provided a new surge of enthusiasm to the effort.

Problems and Progress in OUST's Regional Offices

In the EPA's regional offices, however, it was another story. The six to ten people in a regional OUST program made up a small isolated outpost in a sea of four hundred to fifteen hundred people in each EPA regional office. No one else knew what TQM was, or cared, for that matter. So once trained, the regional employees had to try to apply these concepts in what was, at best, a passive environment and, at worst, a hostile setting. Their colleagues in the region did not understand TQM.

There were occasional reinforcers from headquarters, but they consisted of sending them a book to read, discussions about TQM at quarterly meetings as one topic among many, or participation in some headquarters-led projects where regional or state input or data were needed. This was all far too little to build and sustain a TQM way of working. Looking back, this is an area that called for a more substantial investment of resources. Headquarters needed to make a greater contribution in personal time, effort, teaching, and encouragement to support regional participation. Headquarters should also have pushed harder on asking the regions how they were applying what they had learned in the training.

But a number of separate incidents occurred that made senior management feel that they were succeeding in bringing about the TQM way of thinking and working. For example, one region discussed walking into the underground tank program in Tennessee and being greeted by the program chief, who proudly showed them a series of charts, including run charts on turnaround times for plan approvals and enforcement flow charts. They were immediately able to begin discussing problems and improvements.

OUST's past interactions with the states usually focused on grant paperwork requirements, reporting requirements, and demonstrating the availability of matching state funds and adequate state legislative authority—in other words, mostly bureaucratic tasks that had nothing to do with the actual work of preventing or cleaning up tank leaks. As OUST staff saw change in Tennessee and other states, they began to sense that they could make some fundamental changes in how an environmental regulation and cleanup program was established and implemented.

Early Progress in OUST

By December, when the last class was completed and all OUST people had been through the two-and-a-half-day training, enough positive results were happening to provide additional encouragement. Most OUST employees now recognized and worked to discover and identify "waste," and they were able to eliminate the most egregious forms. For example, the technical branch aggressively worked at using the hotline to respond to inquiries from the public. They limited their involvement to answering only those questions that the hotline could not handle. They worked with the hotline employees to improve their ability to answer the public's questions—recognizing that this investment in teaching would result in a significant savings in time for the technical branch. In another example, Brand asked an administrative assistant about a project she had initiated before we went through the TQM training. "Ron," she said, "we dropped that; we decided it was only going to create waste."

After about a year, the OUST staff called for an intensive session to reinforce their skills and knowledge of TQM work analysis. Cohen, along with other consultants, developed a TQM workshop oriented toward the underground tank program, which culminated with teams deciding to begin a half-dozen new improvement projects. The training retreat was energizing but also identified some problems the organization was having with institutionalizing TQM.

First, some of OUST's senior but nonmanagement employees seemed to believe that TQM meant workplace democracy. In their view, "relying on the experts—the people who do the work" meant that management should simply do whatever the employees advised. On the other side, some of OUST's middle managers had not really accepted the new facilitator role that TQM required of them, ignored many of their employees' better suggestions, and still had the habit of "shooting the messenger." Needless to say, Brand had not entirely succeeded in driving fear from his organization.

An additional issue was that the new way of working was still seen as an "add-on" by some in the organization: they had their "TQM work" and their "regular work." A related issue was that for those in the organization already committed to TQM, they felt management was at fault for moving too slowly to complete the transformation to TQM. Some employees questioned management's commitment and sincerity, since it tolerated a slower learning process than they preferred.

On the positive side, OUST began to use TQM principles and concepts in many aspects of its work. As had happened during the training, the organization's vocabulary changed and stayed changed, which affected behavior. As noted previously, OUST had "allowed" a few of the EPA's other senior managers to attend TQM training sessions. Soon they were using the vocabulary to express themselves and to communicate more directly and effectively, even on topics and programs other than underground tanks.

With the seeds of TQM planted in the OUST organization, Brand then moved to expand OUST's audience to state underground tank organizations. Most of the employees involved in environmental programs in the United States are at the state, county, and municipal or town level. The production system that the federal EPA led involved thousands of loosely connected players at all of these levels. If TQM was to permeate the entire underground tank program, OUST would need to ensure that its state and local counterparts and customers were introduced to these concepts.

At the annual three-day conference for state and regional OUST personnel in Santa Fe, New Mexico, the EPA offered two introductory sessions on TQM. There were many concurrent sessions on technical, legal, and financial subjects of interest to the participants. With about 325 state participants at the conference, we were pleasantly surprised when about 40 people chose to attend each of the sessions. Brand and Cohen conducted these sessions and outlined the principles, demonstrated a few of the tools, and had a couple of state people describe projects they had already completed. One result was a request by states for training in TQM and greater receptivity to the TQM approach in some of OUST's dealings with the states.

As OUST began working with the states on TQM, they noted that many of those directly involved in underground tank cleanup and regulation were private firms. An early success involved the states and the companies that actually did consulting, assessed leaking tank sites, removed tanks, and cleaned up tank leaks. In the past, consultants did what they thought was right or what they thought would meet the minimum standards set by the state. The cleanup plan or soil and water samples would be submitted to the state; months might pass and the answer would be: "This isn't what we want, guess again"; the consultant would take more samples or revise and submit the data or plan again. More time would pass and then more changes would be required. Worse yet, different individuals in the state program would review the package and request something different from what the state had requested earlier.

To address this type of problem, one state decided to hold a consultant's day, to tell the consultants up front what they needed to do. The workload created by hundreds of reported leaks required that the long cycle times for review and the rework by limited state and consultant staff had to be radically reduced.

OUST's regional and headquarters people worked with a number of states to help them create flow charts for their current ad hoc processes and convert these into an agreed-upon state process. They helped the state to develop guidance and simplified forms and procedures. Only then did the state hold its consultant's day. All of this effort over a period of two to four months helped to reduce unnecessary preparation and submissions of forms, samples, site drawings, and other information, which helped the consultant and ultimately the tank owners, who had to pay for everything. It helped the state program by reducing the material to be reviewed, the need to request additional information, and the need to review the same package or site three and four times. The project team viewed this work with the states as a replicable process so that we could help other states conduct consultant's days. Clearly, the savings in workyears and dollars was substantial throughout the system. The team never stopped to quantify the savings, however, but moved on to the next improvement.

Overcoming Obstacles

A flurry of small improvements were made and OUST management felt they were really getting the idea of applying TQM to daily work. Everyone was using the vocabulary and TQM charts showed up more often and in more places. At this time Brand believed that every employee was getting up each morning thinking, "What can I improve today?" But as weeks turned into months, it became clear this was not the case. In retrospect, it is easier to see what was happening at that time.

First, the tank program was innovative and had consistently been recognized for outstanding work. OUST's staff believed that they were applying many of the principles of TQM all along, and although OUST's people knew they could improve further, they felt that the projects they were working on would improve things further. Rather than working toward the highest levels of performance that they could, they settled for doing better than other programs in the agency.

Second, senior management knew that the organization had too many activities going at the same time. This kept OUST from focusing significant resources on a few areas and perpetuated a system of fragmenting people's time and dollar resources among thirty or forty projects, including developing regulations, negotiating grant agreements, and conducting technical studies. OUST used TQM concepts in completing this work, but on an intermittent basis.

Third, although Brand was espousing the TQM approach at every turn, some staff and managers were only giving it lip service and, blaming the pressures of regular work, they continued to work in the old style. Workers knew that Brand wanted TQM approaches and solutions but felt discouraged by their immediate supervisors. The organization's managers and staff had bought into and created a number of innovative processes and solutions before we ever got into TQM. Although Brand preached TQM ad nauseam, he was concerned about overdoing it. Staffers and some of OUST's managers complained that, although OUST was preaching TQM to the states and others, they were not doing enough of it on the organization's own internal work processes. Management said, "Well, what's stopping you? Go ahead and do it." The answer usually was, "We don't have the time," or "The problem is not in my area and I can't tell others what they should do."

At the same time, Brand continued to read in the field and talk with people engaged in TQM in other agencies and companies. Looking back at that period, one of OUST's managers observed, "Ron, we felt like you were constantly hitting us with new ideas and concepts before we achieved a comfort level in using the first set of tools and concepts we were trained in."

So although they were eliminating 30 percent of the data required to be reported by grantees and feeling appropriately good about it, the concept of continuous improvement required more. A number of people in the organization started to fully understand *how* to apply the notion of eliminating inspection at the end of a production process to a regulatory program. Applying this concept in a regulatory program required one to see that many of the reporting requirements that we placed on states were really post hoc inspections that should be eliminated. Brand wanted the reporting of data reduced almost completely. OUST began to understand that simply telling the states to "do better" when they did not know how was not going to improve their performance. It meant that when the states completed fewer enforcement actions or inspections than expected, OUST had to get in there and work with them on improvement projects. The EPA would need to stop the practice of telling states to "do better; do more."

Deciding How Hard to Push

One of the great difficulties OUST management faced at this point was deciding how hard to push for TQM. At times, management held back over worries about being too insistent or dogmatic. Sometimes, it was difficult to tell whether management was being obstinate or persistent. It is important to be sensitive to this issue and to constantly reflect on when to push and when to ease up.

Earlier in OUST's organizational history, when he adopted the franchise approach, Brand's strategy was to refuse to work on an alternative to franchises. An alternative to franchising would have been a fall-back plan that would have allowed the EPA's regional offices to directly operate the program in states that did not apply for delegated authority to run their own underground tank regulatory program. Brand insisted that even to admit that OUST was preparing for such a contingency would encourage states to hold back. This was a high-risk approach, but it worked.

Looking back on the OUST experience, we believe that it is important for top management to play an active and aggressive role in work analysis and improvement projects. Senior managers may fear that their presence in improvement team meetings could inhibit the group's discussions, but although it makes sense to avoid dominating discussions, we believe that senior management should simply recognize the potential problem and overcompensate for it. By not being with the group on at least a few occasions, you miss the opportunity to learn about the obstacles in the process and to do some teaching. Perhaps as important, you can encourage the team to achieve a higher level of improvement than they would otherwise achieve.

Next, we believe it is critical to meet frequently with middle managers to talk about their personal efforts to use the TQM approach. Generally, if a good improvement project or two came out of a shop, Brand assumed the chief was part of the cause, but he later learned that this was frequently not so. In some cases, the manager's contribution consisted of simply permitting it to happen if it did not get in the way of the regular work. In other cases, the manager actively discouraged the TQM approach.

It is also important to hold short sessions with your groups of managers, focusing on one specific topic, for example, reducing cycle time, building quality into a process instead of trying to inspect it in, or getting your staff to identify obstacles to improvement. Although most of OUST management accepted these concepts intellectually, it took time and practice before they were internalized and became part of everything they did.

Cultivating TQM Adherents and Integrating Their Ideas

About four of OUST's nine managers aggressively read and learned more about TQM on their own. Their work and that of their employees frequently reflected the utilization of TQM concepts and tools. But it was as if these were separate islands, or plugs of grass that did not spread to cover the entire lawn.

The workers, or nonsupervisory personnel, also included three or four people who became intensive readers and talkers about TQM. OUST's "TQM talk" sometimes reached a level that others considered obnoxious. OUST's great challenge was to use the enthusiasm and ideas of these employees to shape the organization's regular approach to conducting work.

Reconceptualizing Work in the Underground Tank Program

When we first began OUST, we inherited the traditional approach to achieving environmental change: develop ironclad regulations, enforce them strictly, and demand that states and the regulated community spend money and comply. We soon recognized that both the size of the regulated community (750,000 owners or operators) and the fact that many were small businesses called for a different approach. We learned about TQM just in time to help us make the transition to a new way of working.

Nature of the Work

Much of the work in a relatively new environmental program was process design work in the form of regulations, guidance, procedures, forms, and training. But OUST was at least four or five levels removed from the real work that would actually protect or clean up the environment. For example, let us take the case of a tank owner considering removing a tank or testing it for leaks:

> Level I: The tank owner/operator considers removing or testing a tank.
> Level II: A private company (vendor) is called and plans or takes the necessary action.
> Level III: The state or local agency creates the demand by the tank owner through regulations, outreach, and inspections or enforcement. When the vendor is called in and takes action, the agency applies standards, reviews site plans, and inspects action taken at the site.
> Level IV: The EPA regional staff and headquarters staff (and contractor support) develop policies, regulations, and procedures (and obstacles) for all of the above.
> Level V: Constraints and goals are established by legislation, public expectations, pressure, lobbying groups, previous agency and industry practice, and judicially set precedents.

The traditional approach to developing a new federal regulatory program pays little attention to the needs of players at each of these levels, but we believed that an understanding of the work of people at these levels was critical (Cohen and Kamieniecki, 1991). A positive example of understanding and improving the production process took place when OUST convinced some states to do away with submitting plans for assessing sites where tanks leaked and cleanup was needed. Traditionally, these plans would be reviewed by the states, returned for rework, and eventually submitted to the EPA.

These steps delayed environmental cleanup and in fact caused increased damage as pollution spread out from the original area of contamination. Instead, OUST urged that soil sampling begin immediately and the results be reported, rather than requiring plans for assessing and then cleaning up sites. OUST accomplished this by focusing attention on the program's customers and the need to deliver value-added service to them. Thus conceptualized, one portion of OUST's work became that of speeding up the process of cleaning up leaking tank sites. The time it took to analyze soil samples was no longer a given but an area for potential improvement.

Another part of OUST's work involved its relationship with counterpart offices at the regional and state level. By using TQM methods, OUST improved its review visits to the regions by establishing a process in which the second day of the review focused on addressing an area that needed improvement. For example, where a state's enforcement effort was weak, the entire day would be spent seeking ways to improve it. That day might be the start of a longer regional-state improvement project.

Overall, OUST still spent about 75 percent of its time on internal paperwork related to grants, contracts, reports, meetings, and bureaucratic battles—of which little, if any, was value added. Many of the bureaucratic fights were necessary but not value added as OUST fought to keep the system from creating additional barriers to getting the work done. These battles frequently took six to twelve months and were draining, since they typically involved trying to prevent silly rules, complex financial reporting, and redundant field sampling advocated by lawyers to ensure that future enforcement cases had enough data to overwhelm the courts.

Focus on Field Operations

In retrospect, we believe that OUST would have benefited from an even greater and earlier emphasis on field operations. Basically, we mean all work and decision making that is done away from headquarters, regardless of who has to do it. At some point in your agency's processes, these people have to be viewed as customers. The reason is that you are trying to get them to do something, in a certain way and by a certain time. Government needs this focus on the customer. OUST might have started analyzing broader policy and regulatory issues by finding out what actually happens at Level I. Much of the success OUST had in applying TQM to tank regulation took place when they focused their attention on the field.

OUST's quality improvement teams were most successful when they asked: "What are the causes of the present undesirable practices we want to change or improve?" Many significant improvements took place after project teams had done a cause-and-effect diagram with the real workers at Level I. In those instances, the teams knew specifically what behaviors they were trying to change, or what process they were trying to improve. Too often in government we start at Level IV or V and hope our policies will trickle down to affect real work and workers.

Applying TQM to the Work of a Headquarters Staff Office

At headquarters, we turned the world upside down. Or at least we inverted the organization's chart. We placed headquarters at the bottom and customers at the top, with each level providing support to the group above it. It seems commonplace now, but it helped us all realize we had to work in a different way.

Tank owners
Venders
Local agencies
States
Regions
Headquarters

Analyzing Administrative Work

OUST's policy and program design work required a focus on the field, but producing administrative outputs also benefited from TQM work analysis. OUST started to analyze how they produced regulations, memos, and letters to Congress. Quality teams looked at the organization's project tracking system, the methods used for processing travel authorizations and reimbursements, the way the organization developed its budget, and even the way telephones were covered. Over and over again staff identified waste, including rework, unnecessary inspections, and non-value-added work. In the end, OUST improved productivity by removing waste and improving quality.

Analyzing External Customers' Needs

A number of OUST's employees were deeply involved in providing tools to assist field operations. The branch in OUST responsible for analyzing technology and providing tools for technical field tasks, such as leak detection and cleanup, was one of the first units to integrate TQM into their regular work. They began by examining the work in their existing inventory, and they quickly identified work in the non-value-added categories like rework and unnecessary work and tried to eliminate it.

Sometimes they went too far, on one occasion proposing that they stop responding to routine congressional inquiries. When that type of suggestion comes from employees, it is management's job to say, "No, we do that work because it is part of our political process." Additionally, in this particular case it is a misunderstanding about the concept of customer, for certainly the legislative branch of government was a key customer of the underground tank program. An employee's assertion that a certain type of work is waste must be treated as a suggestion and not a decision.

In the past, OUST employees decided to do projects that they thought were important and then tried to sell them to others. Now, experience and feedback showed that the resulting products were not being used. To change this, they attacked the customer diagnosis part of their own project development process. In a few intense sessions, the branch developed a one-page format that described a proposed project, its intended purpose, and who was supposed to benefit. Along with this, they developed a checkbox questionnaire, which asked the reader to comment on the proposed project. Some of the questions were

> How often do you do this work?
> Would you use the project or product in the field?
> Should we accelerate the project, or "drop the whole thing"?

This questionnaire went out to people in the state and local agencies who worked at sites and the field staff of companies that responded to tank release calls.

Working with Customers to Develop New "Products"

In another aspect of the work, the states told OUST they wanted a uniform lab method for assessing samples from leaking tank sites. OUST kept trying to get them to radically decrease the number of samples they were taking and processing, but the project team met with representatives of six state programs and it was clear that they were not ready to take such a step. After listening to the customer, OUST supported a project led by the states to see if they could identify and agree on a common lab protocol for such samples. The resources allocated to this project included employee time and a small number of contract dollars. After several months of work, the project team concluded that they could not produce a common protocol. The important thing here is that OUST did not try to argue them out of it but worked with the customer to give it a fair trial.

Meanwhile, the organization worked on a number of quality improvement projects, keeping in mind that the program was primarily dealing with leaking gasoline tanks, rather than the unknown set of substances involved in a toxic waste cleanup. The people working in the gasoline tank cleanup field were transferring beliefs and practices from the hazardous waste and Superfund programs where they had to be concerned with specifically identifying the type of chemicals in the soil, air, or water. But as one staffer said, "Hey, this is gasoline; you can see it, smell it, taste it. Get started cleaning it up. The longer you take to analyze it, the more opportunity it has to spread."

With this thinking, the employees began to concentrate on projects that would reduce the time and expense involved in defining and cleaning up the contaminated area. How was this different from the way OUST had been working? How did TQM affect the organization? Although the staff generally had been concerned with these issues, TQM sharpened the focus and made them almost fanatical in enabling people in the field to do the needed work. TQM forced OUST to look at the entire field-level process and engendered a close working relationship with industry to develop faster, simpler methods of cleaning up contamination.

For example, OUST worked with industry to accelerate development of a method known as "lab-in-the-bag." OUST staff developed methods of instruction, including videos, so that state agencies could use and understand the new method. But most important, the EPA needed them to accept the use of this simpler method, so the project team treated each link in the chain as a customer. They needed to get the vendor to design an appropriate tool, the state agency to permit its use, and the consultants and environmental firms to accept and use it. If any one of these customer groups did not buy in, OUST could not accomplish its goal of simpler, faster, less-expensive cleanup. No one was saying that this improvement was someone else's job: all knew OUST had to assist at any point in the development or distribution chain if it wanted this to have a chance of succeeding. As it was, it took a two-year period to bring this about, and even today, it has been put in place in some states but others have yet to adopt it.

Learning to Accept the Uneven Rate of Progress

There were constant "ups and downs" during the first three years of implementing TQM. For example, the EPA regional staff reported that a state had just been given fifteen additional positions to add to a minimal group of five devoted to the tank program in that state. This was great news. Then the region pointed out that the program director was swamped with current work. She would not have time to recruit, develop position descriptions, and complete the bureaucratic work necessary to fill those positions. When HQ asked what they were going to do to help her, the regional staff were puzzled and did not know.

This was a constant problem. In our view, anytime you want to get someone to do something, you should look at them as a customer. That means asking yourself what you can do to help the customer take the action you want. In this case, OUST wanted more employees assigned to the state tank program. The legislature had acted, but the program chief did not have the time to complete the action to get the new people on board. In such a situation, the regional office should have aggressively worked with her to help get position descriptions written, recruitment actions started, applicants screened—whatever it took. This was outside the normal work done by the EPA regions, but it needed to be done.

In some cases, there were dramatic improvements in quality and in cost savings throughout the production process, but in other cases, normal bureaucratic inertia dominated efforts to improve work processes. One of the most difficult things to accept is that early on you will see a number of TQM failures at quality improvement; it is important to remember, however, that before you started thinking about this new way of working you were "failing" and did not even know it.

Perhaps the most difficult thing to explain is how the cumulative effect of using TQM concepts and tools affected the broader aspects of the office's work. The organization constantly fought over making things simpler and easier to use. If Brand, as chief, lagged or slipped, the employees would quickly remind him that he was not working in a TQM way. Because of the way OUST employees used the TQM lessons, they were usually better informed about the real work, the way it was done, the customer's needs, and the supplier's realistic capabilities. It was important to understand that you can only improve from where you are, and therefore, you need to make it okay to clearly identify the present level of performance, even when it is poor.

When faced with what sometimes appeared to be impossible goals set by Congress or the EPA's own leadership, OUST tried to honestly develop a means of meeting them. If this could not be done, the flow chart, the fishbone, and customer diagnoses became an important means of educating and communicating with others. OUST project teams presented a flow chart that showed why a process would take eighteen months when someone in Congress or "upstairs" was insisting that the job be done in twelve months. Then the team asked for suggestions on how to improve the process. Since the team usually did its homework well, it was not easy to improve on the design. As a result, OUST helped make other people's expectations more realistic, which made it easier for everyone (regions, states, vendors, and tank owners) to concentrate on getting the job done.

This was very different from the programs where huge amounts of time and energy went toward explaining why they were not meeting someone else's expectations. Brand remembers one meeting that was attended by a number of program directors. Upset by some unrealistic expectations (set by superiors) that were diverting them from their work and driving them to distraction, they asked, "How are you getting away with this? How are you getting away with setting expectations instead of having others set them for you?"

We believe that TQM forced OUST to concentrate on the customer and the real work. If you keep looking at the entire process and finding out how it really works, and enlist employees' help in improving it, you are in a unique position. You set the frame of reference and determine what can be accomplished and how long it will take. Only you know your system's capability. Working in this way gives you and your organization a tremendous sense of competence and confidence. You tackle things that others consider impossible to change or achieve, and sometimes you do the impossible. When you do this in support of your customers and suppliers, they, in turn, support you instead of acting as adversaries.

One of the major indicators of success in the underground tank program is that the EPA was able to put in place a new national regulatory and cleanup program that had tangible results in the field in a short period of time (Cohen and Kamieniecki, 1991). An effective state-federal team identified tens of thousands of tanks where a release was indicated. Appropriate action was undertaken to correct these problems and to eliminate environmental and health hazards. In the EPA's federal role, the program focused on helping the other frontline players doing environmental work, constantly trying to minimize the red tape and other obstacles. The EPA also provided resources to state governments to clean up tank system leaks when private parties were unable or unwilling to do so.

From a management perspective, a critical indicator of OUST's success was that the program operated with only forty people in headquarters and about eighty in the EPA's ten regional offices. This contrasts quite favorably with similar programs in the EPA. By governmental standards, the EPA's underground tank organization is tiny. In our view, the fact that OUST designed and implemented a national program like this while limiting the size of the federal staff, and even decreasing it over time, may be one of the most important indicators of OUST's success in working with TQM.

We have told this story to try to provide a concrete perspective on the difficulties of implementing TQM. Chapter Eight provides a number of TQM success stories from OUST and from other government agencies, indicating that TQM has succeeded in a variety of public organizations. The Office of Underground Storage Tanks is certainly not unique, and TQM can be implemented in any governmental organization.

CHAPTER 8

TQM Success Stories

At this point we hope we have demonstrated that, though it is not easy, TQM can be brought into a governmental organization. Chapter Seven provides details on the struggle to implement TQM at one small office in the federal government. This chapter discusses some examples from government organizations that have used TQM to improve their own performance. Every day this story is rewritten as additional successes accumulate.

We should note that there are also a number of failures. Some organizations have taken on the form but not the substance of TQM. Others have tried but failed at efforts to improve specific types of performance. In baseball, an all-star is someone who gets a hit three out of ten times at bat. One should not be surprised if government fails to bat 1.000 at TQM. Although we have deliberately omitted discussions of failed TQM projects in this chapter, let us assure you that we have observed them as well. Sometimes improvement projects fail because they are poorly designed or poorly selected; at other times, our best and most creative efforts simply lead us down a blind alley. In our view, these success stories demonstrate that TQM can work. We have found no organizational type or work process that cannot be improved by using a quality approach.

Success Story Number 1: The Case of Annual Guidance to the Field

We will provide a number of examples from other organizations, but we will start with two from the organization that we worked with, the Office of Underground Storage Tanks (OUST) of the United States Environmental Protection Agency (US EPA) (this case is described in detail in Chapter Seven). We believe that the best way to learn quality management is to try it, and the best way to write about it is to relay one's own experiences.

Each year, one of OUST's branches is expected to issue annual guidance to the EPA's ten regional offices, located throughout the United States, and to state governments. This annual operating guidance establishes priorities for preventing releases from and cleaning up leaking underground storage tanks and delineates procedures for accomplishing the EPA's environmental goals. Although it is an important assignment, it is one that the staff always dreads, and it is usually assigned to the newest, least experienced member of the staff.

The reason that the assignment is avoided is that traditionally it has required a frustrating series of drafts, discussions, and meetings on what should be included in the document. Management gave little clear direction on the emphasis or importance of the document. In the year before this story, the staff person assigned to produce the guidance suffered through three months—from the day she received the assignment to a completed, approved, and issued operating guidance. It started with a sketchy outline from her boss on what had to be done and a suggestion to talk to the staff person who worked on the guidance the previous year. Quickly she decided that there had to be a better way, so on her own she began by identifying the steps involved in completing the guidance. She included the steps taken to learn how to produce the guidance and the work required to actually complete the document. She talked with those who had to supply portions of it and the users or customers who received it. Then, to display the information, she developed a flow chart of the process that she and others had undertaken to complete the guidance.

Her next step was to look at the work process that she had just undertaken and identify steps that could be shortened or eliminated. She produced a "before-and-after" flow chart, describing the current process and outlining a new, streamlined process. At a meeting with Brand she demonstrated a computer disk she had produced that included the "after" flow chart and explained the procedures that must be followed to complete the guidance. The disk also had easy-to-follow instructions on whom to collect information from, how to get field input and reaction, and at what points in the process to obtain management approval. The latest guidance was also included on the disk, since each year's operating guidance is essentially an update of the previous year's.

This improvement project did not bear fruit until the following year. But when a new person was assigned the task of updating the guidance the following year, she used the disk and instructions successfully to

- Shorten the process for completing the operating guidance
- Reduce the amount of employee time required to produce the guidance
- Improve the quality of the guidance (since everyone knew the standard process and how and when to make their contribution)
- Improve morale, as friction was reduced because a well-structured process prevented this from becoming the annual "crisis" project that everyone loves to hate

As we have indicated throughout this book, a central concept of quality management is that of serving the customer. Customers are not simply external parties who pay money for a product but people both inside and outside your organization who use and rely on the things you produce. In this case there are a number of customers for the product produced by this improvement project. First is the unknown person who will be given this assignment next year. Second are the managers of the Office of Underground Storage Tanks who had simply reacted piecemeal to this annual annoyance. The employee had improved a process that everyone had accepted as a given, and by so doing she had educated her supervisors. The third consists of the people who use and distribute the guidance. Clarifying the process makes it possible to get it done on time. A well-understood set of operating procedures enables OUST to reduce the hassle of issuing the guidance and makes it possible to build on the previous year's guidance and produce a higher-quality set of guidelines for use by staff in the EPA's regional offices and counterpart offices in the states.

The process did not require an elaborate quantitative analysis or a great deal of staff time. However, by allowing a staff person the freedom to question and examine the work process, OUST management released a creative force that resulted in a more efficient, more effective product. Notice also that although she did not create a formal team, she worked with suppliers, customers, and others involved in the process and used the flow chart as her basic tool for communication and revision.

Success Story Number 2: Working with Suppliers

In this case, the suppliers are the engineering consulting firms that clean up leaks from underground gasoline tanks. The program that Ronald Brand directed in the EPA has two jobs: one is to ensure that state and local governments prevent leaks from underground petroleum and chemical storage tanks; the second is to ensure that when tanks do leak, the environmental damage is cleaned up. This case deals with the latter program—environmental cleanup. When tanks leak, the tank owner—usually a gasoline station operator—must hire a contractor to clean up the damage caused by the leak. Under federal cleanup regulations, before a cleanup begins, the government (either the federal government or more frequently, under delegation, the state government) must review and approve a cleanup plan.

In one midwestern state the cleanup process was being held up by delays in approving cleanup plans. Everyone was frustrated. The state officials were deluged with phone calls and paperwork, cleanup plans were piling up in their in-boxes, and plans were repeatedly returned to cleanup contractors for revisions. Meanwhile the gas stations with leaking tanks were shut down and could not be operated, which, of course, made it difficult for the tank owner to earn the money needed to pay for cleaning up the leak.

"Jack Cleanheart," the head of the state tank program, was ready to quit the government due to the constant turmoil and pressure. Jack was quite relieved when the federal EPA called to discuss a project to improve relations with cleanup contractors. The project was to organize a consultant's day for all the contractors that conduct petroleum and gasoline clean-ups within the state. The purpose of the day was to facilitate communication between the state agency and the cleanup firms.

To prepare for the consultant's day, the federal EPA worked with the state to clarify what they expected from con-tractors. Since the EPA had helped organize these events in some other states, they were able to help the state anticipate the type of questions contractors would ask. Another early step in planning a consultant's day was to brainstorm about the barri-ers faced by contractors attempting to meet the state's require-ments. One of the first steps taken by the state was to develop a flow chart that illustrated the steps that took place from the moment an underground tank leak was reported until the time a cleanup actually began.

Jack and his co-workers were surprised when they discov-ered that each of them did the work in a different way. It took some staff one day and others one month to review the same type of plan. They learned that each used different criteria in approving the placement of wells used to monitor soil contami-nation. They applied different decision rules in approving the type of equipment to be used during cleanup. They even differed on which environmental permits the contractor would need to obtain in order to begin the cleanup. They did not have any written procedures or guidelines governing the review of cleanup plans, and thus each review was unique. The process of preparing for a consultant's day made it clear to the staff why contractors were confused and upset. Each cleanup plan had to be reworked many times because the agency was not sure about what they wanted.

Before a consultant's day could take place, Jack realized his organization would need to develop a set of guidelines and standard procedures for reviewing cleanup plans. Jack and his staff began by looking at each step in the process of reporting a leak and submitting a cleanup plan. For example, what type of information did the state really need from firms reporting leaks? How did the agency staffer record the information when it came in over the phone? Should the agency develop a standard form for recording leaks, describing the data needed? If the agency developed a standard form, why not give it to the contractor to gather and report the right information in the first place?

The state decided to develop a standard leak report form, but with each staff member used to requiring the data he or she preferred, it was not easy to get agreement on what the form should include. However, with effort and the assistance of a facilitator, eventually a form was designed that played an important role in the work process. It clarified for the agency and its suppliers (the contractors) what the state expected. It reduced variation in the processes of reporting leaks and saved everyone the waste and frustration of reporting the same leak several times. Jack then turned to the other key steps in the cleanup process and attempted to reach agreement on those steps as well.

Jack began to understand the difficulty contractors faced when interacting with his organization, and he decided that before he held a consultant's day it would be wise to meet with a small number of contractors for some informal conversations. His facilitator recommended convening a focus group—a small number of people who were both customers and suppliers in the process—to test some themes for the consultant's day. The focus group session identified specific problems that contractors had with the state's requirements and provided an indication of the high degree of frustration and anger felt by the contractors over state practices. They were upset because the lack of a clear process was costing them money. Redoing plans and cleanup activities was expensive. The contractors were worried about the ability of their customers, mainly small businesses, to absorb the costs of cleanup.

Using the practical questions and proposed solutions generated by the focus group, Jack's staff continued to clarify and streamline their procedures. The decision to hold the consultant's day became the catalyst in improving the agency's operations. When the session was held it was a great success, with over 150 contractors in attendance. The staff felt confident because they had anticipated almost all the questions and had answers based on a clear and simple set of procedures they had developed.

The state had developed and communicated a clear set of expectations of the contractors that supplied cleanup services. They devoted substantial resources to the critical TQM principle of working with suppliers. Bear in mind that the state did not simply hand down an edict to contractors. It worked with the EPA and a focus group to identify supplier needs and capabilities, and based on what it learned from this group, it further modified the process. It then allocated scarce resources to a day to explain state requirements to the contractors. Communication efforts did not end on consultant's day; in fact, communication with suppliers built on the work done to prepare for the day. Many of the handouts used on consultant's day are now routinely used to answer questions posed by new suppliers and by tank owners with leaking tanks.

Success Story Number 3: Sacramento Air Logistics Center of the U.S. Air Force

In 1991, the Federal Quality Institute gave the air force's Sacramento Air Logistics Center (SM-ALC) a "Quality Improvement Prototype Award." The Air Force Logistics Command began a TQM program in late 1987 and according to the

Federal Quality Institute had one of the best TQM programs in the federal government. According to the air force, the SM-ALC has supported a dramatic improvement in air mission capability: "Not long ago, only 40 percent of Air Force F-11 fighter planes could get airborne at any given time. At the end of 1988 this mission capability rate had risen to 74 percent. Today [1991] it is over 76 percent and still rising. Likewise, the A-10 attack aircraft currently has a mission capability rate of 88.3 percent. This figure is the highest ever for this aircraft and the best in the Air Force" (Federal Quality Institute, 1991, p. 12).

The improvements noted by the air force report were accomplished through a number of small-scale improvement projects. We quote again from the report: "Over the past five years, SM-ALC has had over 264 different process improvement teams. The teams have included formal process action teams, as well as informal quality circles and adhoc groups" (Federal Quality Institute, 1991, p. 12).

The report summarizes some of the accomplishments of these improvement teams, including the following three examples:

1. "*Problem:* Fuel leaks were occurring in F-111 aircraft internal fuel tanks after de-sealing and resealing operations. The delivery of fourteen aircraft was delayed because of leaks. *Action:* Develop a new method to seal tanks using high pressure water rather than chemical solvents. *Results:* It now takes three days longer to de-seal the tanks, but leaks have been reduced from an average of 5.3 per aircraft to 3.0. There were no delivery delays in the first thirty-seven aircraft after the process improvement. . . ."

2. "*Problem:* Off-base contractors desiring access to the base had to spend an average of twenty-two minutes to complete security processing. *Action:* Eliminate requirements for unnecessary and redundant information. Reduce duplicate files and forms. *Results:* Security processing now takes less than eight minutes. We have realized savings of a thousand man-hours per year. . . ."

3. "*Problem:* Delinquent contract deliveries had reached almost 4,000 line items in January 1988. *Action:* Revise proce-

dures for processing purchase requests and following up on contract deliveries. Provide additional training for contract administrators. *Results:* Delinquent deliveries dropped to 678— an 83 percent reduction—by September 1990" (Federal Quality Institute, 1991, p. 12).

Success Story Number 4: The Case of the Overdrafted Memo

For soon-to-be-obvious reasons, this TQM success story will remain anonymous. In a large municipal government in the Northeast, one particular office was having great difficulty meeting deadlines. The office served as a policy analysis shop for the commissioner of a local consumer protection agency. The director of the office was a former professor who was widely acknowledged to be a creative, if not brilliant, analyst and strategist. Unfortunately, he also had the reputation of being someone who was never on time for a meeting and never delivered an assignment on schedule.

Naturally, his staff found this to be quite frustrating and realized that their own effectiveness was impaired by the reputation their boss had as the "absent-minded professor." One of the newer members of the staff had developed an interest in TQM, and she convinced the boss to read a few articles on the subject. After a few weeks, the boss decided to hire a consultant to lead a one-day TQM training session and retreat. Upon returning to the office, four of the senior analysts asked if they could form a quality improvement team to tackle the office's problem with missed deadlines.

One of the first tasks that the team took on was to chart the office's last twenty-five assignments from the commissioner. They tracked the amount of time it took from the moment the assignment was initiated. They developed flow charts identifying each step taken to respond to the assignment, who completed each task, and how long it took to complete the project.

Their analysis discovered that the average assignment took fourteen working days to complete and was four days late. They learned that 75 percent of their assignments required a memo as the primary media of response, 12 percent required a longer report, and 13 percent required an oral briefing. They decided to focus their attention initially on the process of producing memos since that was the type of medium in which they tended to communicate.

Further analysis discovered that a first draft of a memo in response to the assignment was normally completed in 2.5 days. But they documented that an average of 7.5 drafts were completed prior to the deadline. Clearly the problem was either in the process of providing initial instructions to those writing the memos or in the quality and specificity of the comments. It turned out that only one person seemed to reject draft memos more than twice—the boss. In fact, if the boss's review was eliminated, the entire problem of late performance would be eliminated.

The improvement team decided to test whether the boss had been listening during the part of the TQM training that had dealt with driving out fear from the workplace. They set up a meeting with the boss to discuss the results of their analysis. After a difficult and intense three-hour session, the boss agreed to a new procedure. A new assignment sheet was drawn up to attempt to elicit a more complete set of instructions from the boss regarding the memo's purpose and content. Second, the improvement team would develop a new cover sheet for memos that indicated what draft the memo was in and when the memo was due and provided a deadline for comments. Informally, the boss agreed to try to reduce the number of drafts he required before approving a memo as final.

After a month under the new procedures, the staff felt that some improvement had taken place and decided to conduct an analysis of the past month's new assignments. Their analysis discovered that the average assignment took eleven working days to complete and was 1.5 days late. Although no one believed that the improvement process was over, everyone was pleased with the improvement. Encouraged by this beginning success, the improvement team met again to try to eliminate missed assignments.

Success Story Number 5: Productivity Gains Through Employee Participation at the New York City Department of Sanitation

The New York City Department of Sanitation's vehicle maintenance division was plagued with problems when Ronald Contino arrived (Contino and Giuliano, 1991). On any given day, half the vehicles were out of service and one-third of those that did leave the garage broke down before the end of the run. With sixty shops spread throughout the city, supervision of employees was minimal. Any improvement would require the support and involvement of all levels of workers and management.

Contino attacked the problems on several fronts. He brought in a number of new employees who understood his goals for the organization and proceeded to seek out and place in key positions people already in the division who had potential and were not afraid of change. A management information system was set up to measure the efficiency and effectiveness of performance. At that point, he was prepared to focus on worker involvement.

Contino set up a labor team, but he wanted to avoid the traditional formal agreements that, in his mind, made such cooperative efforts ineffective and virtually meaningless. He presented his plan to the unions as completely voluntary, so that both he and the labor representatives were free to leave at any time. Members of the labor team, representing the various trades in the division, had to be approved by both the union leadership and Contino.

The labor team had three goals. The first was communication. It was important for information not to be filtered by the existing levels of bureaucracy, because distortion developed as information traveled both from top to bottom and bottom to top. The labor team members served as conduits from the workers to Contino, and both sides would benefit from the access. The second goal was to improve the quality of work life. Contino believed that if the work environment became more hospitable, morale and productivity would also improve. The final goal was to solve the operating problems of the division. The workers are the experts on what takes place in the garages, they know what does not work, and they often have suggestions for solving problems.

As the labor team identified problems and concerns, Contino worked with them to implement solutions. He directed them to work through the system to make changes, but he kept his door open as a final arbiter in the event of conflict. He instructed management to work with the labor team and to refrain from hindering the improvement process.

One of the first results was the improvement of working conditions in the garage: lighting was improved immediately, the heating systems were repaired, and maintenance on the buildings themselves was increased. This served to build trust among the workers and demonstrated that management was serious about working with them and solving problems. Over time, other improvements were made, such as installation of air conditioning and the purchase of exercise equipment.

The workers offered a number of suggestions for reducing vehicle downtime. Much of the delay existed because the garages either had to wait for spare parts to arrive from the borough shop or because they did not have the proper equipment. Many jobs required only a couple of hours of labor but resulted in vehicles being down for days. The labor team asked for the proper tools so that more of the work could be done in the garages, instead of the borough shop, and also suggested revamping of the supply system, allowing the garages to have more parts on hand. This way, less work would be delayed by waiting for runners to pick up and deliver parts from the borough shops.

The importance of involving unions and adjusting participation to the local organization's historical pattern is illustrated by the following quote from union representative John Giuliano:

> Prior to Ron Contino, it was "them versus us."
> Management did not care about us, and we worked
> like pigs in pigsties. Morale was low. There were

hundreds of grievances. The union was fighting
management every day. . . . We were not telling
management about problems repairing their
trucks until Ron Contino came along with the
concept of involving the work force. He ap-
proached the union leadership. We figured, "Let
us give his plan a shot; we can always go back to the
way we were."

The guidelines were that no labor team member would get involved in union matters regarding
discipline or grievances. One key point to this
agreement was that it was on a handshake. Nothing was written down. Either party could walk out
the door. Another key point was that no one would
lose a job. We would put the organization on its
feet together and get more efficient [Contino and
Giuliano, 1991, p. 189].

Success Story Number 6: Quality Improvements at the Department of Veterans Affairs

Managers at the Philadelphia Regional Office of the Department of Veterans affairs began experimenting with TQM when
they realized that there was a real need to improve the quality
of services that the agency provides to veterans and other
beneficiaries. In the past, the department had based its operations on "internally derived service standards" (Koons, 1991,
p. 35) that did not necessarily reflect the priorities and concerns of the agency's customers (veterans and beneficiaries). In
the past, no real attempts had been made to clearly define customer interests or examine internal operating processes to see
whether or not they satisfied customer expectations and needs.

One of the functions that the agency decided to examine
was the process by which the agency gave loans to veterans
against their insurance policies. It is both interesting and
instructive to note that, prior to examining this process in
terms of customer needs, agency staff felt that they were providing excellent service. The agency's goal had been to process

loan requests within five business days. After talking to veterans, the staff realized that, even if the agency *always* met its processing goals of five days, it still took two full weeks for policy holders to receive loan checks once they had filled out applications. This extra delay was built into the system, since it took several days for the application to arrive at the agency by mail, three or four days for the Treasury Department to process the check, a few more days to send the check back through the mail, and a few weekends in between. So, from the policy holder's perspective, the loan process took two full weeks.

When agency staff examined this process from the standpoint of the policy holders, they realized that two weeks was too long, since any veteran or beneficiary who was applying for a loan against an insurance policy probably needed the money quickly. Instead of accepting the fact that two weeks was the best they could do, agency staff began looking for ways to trim wasted time from the process.

They began by setting up a fax machine so that policy holders had the option of faxing applications instead of mailing them. This option was accompanied by a guarantee that the agency would process applications on the same day they received them. An additional improvement was made when the agency began renting an inexpensive post office box especially for loan applications, which has resulted in speedier mail delivery. Under the new system, the mail is picked up every morning by 5:30 and delivered to the office by 6:00 A.M. so that the applications are ready for processing by 8:00 A.M., when the office opens. Simply by implementing these two improvements, turnaround time for application processing has been cut to 1.6 workdays.

This case is an excellent example of the gap that can often be found between a service provider's standards and a customer's expectations. The staff at this agency felt that they were doing an excellent job until they actually asked their customers about their real needs. Even in circumstances where the vast majority of customers are satisfied, there can still be a great deal of room for improvement. In describing his agency's efforts to improve service, Paul Koons cautions other managers about fooling themselves with numbers: "For example, if a satisfaction survey reports that 97 percent of the respondents are 'satisfied' with the service provided, there may be a tendency to say or think that the organization is doing great. What it actually may be saying when you apply the percentages to the total universe of those you serve is that there is a large group of individuals who were not satisfied with the service they received. In the case of our toll-free unit which receives over 600,000 calls a year, a 97 percent satisfaction rating means that approximately 18,000 callers were not satisfied" (Koons, 1991, p. 36).

Success Story Number 7: Blount Memorial Hospital in Maryville, Tennessee

Administrative errors, rework, time delays, and process variation are frustrating and costly in public-sector organizations. They can be life threatening in hospitals and public health agencies, a life-and-death urgency that may be one of the reasons why the health services industry has been particularly quick to embrace TQM. Thus, when Joseph Dawson became the chief administrator at Blount Memorial Hospital (BMH) in Maryville, Tennessee, he began his TQM efforts by assessing the hospital's current state as well as community needs and expectations. The hospital had suffered heavy financial losses, including a burdensome long-term debt. In addition, BMH had a declining admissions rate, a brand new board of directors, and a steadily deteriorating relationship with the community (Matherly and Lasater, 1992, p. 82).

Following an off-site retreat for administrators, TQM training began for the hospital administrator, all assistant administrators, and all division and department heads. After everyone had received training, TQM projects were initiated in almost every area of the hospital's operations. The projects were very diverse, ranging from a new program designed to reduce the number of false fire alarms to a project aimed at reducing the number of billing errors.

The staff in BHM's admissions department undertook a project that examined the staff's accuracy in transcribing employer information from patient admitting or information forms. After an initial analysis, the staff determined that there was a 6.5 percent error rate associated with transferring information from one form to the other. This was deemed too high by the project team and the staff began a series of meetings regarding the processing of forms and the coding system. After agreeing that ambiguities in the coding system were primarily to blame for the error rate, appropriate changes were made in the coding procedure and the error rate fell to less than 1 percent.

Positive changes have occurred in other areas at BMH that are clearly attributable to TQM: customer satisfaction levels have risen, the quality of work has improved, costs have been lowered, absenteeism is down, safety and morale have improved, and the employee turnover rate is lower.

Success Story Number 8: Defense Contract Management District Northeast

In the past several years, there has been a dramatic decline in the Defense Department's budget. This type of lean fiscal environment has challenged organizations like the Defense Contract Management District Northeast (DCMD Northeast) to streamline its operating procedures in order to continue to accomplish its goals and objectives. DCMD Northeast's principal mission is to manage the Defense Department's contracts with outside entities and to ensure that defense contractors are providing high-quality products and services.

The DCMD Northeast has 3,895 employees who oversee 82,588 defense contracts worth over $150 billion with 4,477 suppliers throughout the Northeast (Federal Quality Institute, 1992a, pp. ii, 1). To manage this high volume of information and material more effectively, DCMD Northeast set out to eliminate all communication barriers between customers and suppliers. In creating a strategy for the implementation of TQM, DCMD Northeast's executive steering committee developed its own organizational philosophy: "To create and maintain an environment that promotes customer satisfaction through teamwork and continuous process improvement." With over 4,477 suppliers, effective customer-supplier communication is absolutely essential.

When DCMD Northeast began its agencywide TQM program in 1988, manufacturing costs were rising and product quality was declining. The costs of rework, errors, and repairs were becoming intolerably high. DCMD Northeast began by asking contractors to examine their manufacturing and assembly processes in order to improve efficiency and reduce mistakes and at the same time began efforts to communicate its needs as a customer more effectively. One important result of the improved communication was that it became possible to actually change manufacturing specifications, instead of simply paying for and accepting inferior products. This would have been unthinkable before TQM.

Implementing TQM at DCMD Northeast has been a long and laborious process, but the organization has begun to enjoy some significant improvements. Two of the most important indicators managers at DCMD Northeast use to monitor performance are product quality and database integrity (Federal Quality Institute, 1992a).

Between 1989 and 1991, DCMD Northeast managed to dramatically improve supplier communication and coordination efforts. By working closely with Navy customers and contractors, for example, DCMD Northeast reduced the reject rate of crucial piping systems and submarine hull materials from 10.7 percent to 7.5 percent.

This type of communication between contractors and DCMD Northeast has resulted in fewer products that fail to meet contract specifications. In 1988, DCMD Northeast and the contractors established a formal process whereby specifications, priorities, and goals are agreed on (prior to the start of the manufacturing process) in memoranda of agreement (MOA), which has reduced reject rates for several contractors by up to 53 percent. One contractor was able to reduce the rework rate by 48 percent.

Another performance indicator is database integrity. As the DCMD Northeast currently administers over 80,000 contracts, effective management requires that a large portion of contract information be stored in computerized databases; thus, the accuracy of the data input process is extremely important. Between May 1989 and May 1991, a process action team studied data entry methods and made several important recommendations, which reduced the error rate for delivery-schedule records by about 80 percent. For supply-line records, they reduced the error rate from 19.1 percent to 6.1 percent.

Since implementing TQM in 1988, DCMD Northeast employees have made 325 improvement recommendations, some very minor, but others, like those noted previously, with major impacts. DCMD Northeast credits TQM with saving the organization over $1 million during the last two fiscal years, and in 1992, the Federal Quality Institute awarded DCMD Northeast a Quality Improvement Prototype Award.

Success Story Number 9: Public Services and Administration, Patent and Trademark Office, Department of Commerce, Arlington, Virginia

Another 1992 Quality Improvement Prototype Award winner is the Public Services and Administration (PSA), one of the six organizations that make up the Patent and Trademark Office in Arlington, Virginia. PSA itself has eight offices, employs 750 people, and has a budget of approximately $70 million. PSA began a quality improvement program in 1989, after identifying several major problems (Federal Quality Institute, 1992c).

- The workload had increased dramatically from 1981 to 1989. Patent application filings were up 42 percent and trademark filings had increased by 51 percent.
- Past work processes had emphasized quantity (of applications processed) over quality.
- The rework and error rates were extremely high.
- The employee turnover rate was 24 percent in fiscal year 1989.
- The number of customer complaints and employee grievances had increased significantly.

- PSA's standard operating processes were outdated and inefficient.

After evaluating these and other problems at PSA, senior management decided to implement TQM. It is both interesting and instructive to note that the senior managers avoided blindly following any particular TQM guru or quality consultant. Instead, they studied several different approaches and integrated those elements that they found useful into a coherent strategy for their own organization.

One of the first action plans developed by PSA managers focused on dealing with the changes that were sure to result as quality improvement became embedded in PSA's organizational culture. Senior managers elicited involvement from managers, supervisors, and frontline employees in developing plans for "union involvement, training, recognition, customer focus, and employee teams" (Federal Quality Institute, 1992c, p. 8). There is no separate or formal quality organization at PSA but rather, the responsibility for product quality and customer satisfaction belongs to everyone.

In pursuing the goal of customer satisfaction, PSA embarked on a campaign to place the organization's focus squarely on the customer. Since PSA employees were not accustomed to thinking in terms of "customers," focus workshops were held in each work unit in order to identify the unit's customers and the products and services that the organization provides for them, as well as customer needs and expectations in terms of products and services. These focus groups were extremely useful, as they helped employees learn their roles in the quality equation.

PSA has been working with TQM since 1989 and has made significant improvements in a number of important processing areas. One such area involves the mailing of receipts to patent applicants. The agency's goal, in the late 1980s, was to mail filing receipts to applicants no later than twenty-two days after receiving completed applications. In fact, applicants were receiving filing receipts approximately thirty-six to thirty-eight days after actually filing and some were forced to wait up to sixty days. After making a flow chart of the application filing process, a review team streamlined the procedure, eliminating unnecessary steps, restructuring work units, instituting a "one-stop" processing system, retraining employees, and establishing a feedback process in order to evaluate performance. As a result, the agency's new goal level of eighteen days (within which to send filing receipts to applicants) was reached in fiscal year 1991. Also, the error rate associated with the filing of receipts was reduced by over 50 percent and customer requests for corrections were reduced by 81 percent. The reconfiguration of this process resulted in an annual savings of about $40,000 for the agency.

Another improvement project focused on assignment recordation. Assignments are documents that identify owners of patents and trademarks. The recording of assignments is an integral function of the Patent and Trademark Office, and the accuracy and timeliness of recordation is extremely important, since business decisions worth millions of dollars are often made based on patent ownership information. The agency's stated goal for processing an assignment recordation was 20 days; the *actual* time that it was taking, however, was over 100 days.

A process review team undertook a review and eliminated non-value-added work, identified the causes of errors, improved staff knowledge of available technology, standardized the process, and conducted customer focus sessions. As a result, the agency has managed to meet its goal of twenty processing days, and customer complaints have dropped by 50 percent. Managers estimate that the agency has saved approximately 7,000 workhours per year.

A third significant improvement was made in mail processing. The Patent and Trademark Office receives approximately 30,000 pieces of mail every day, each of which must be read, sorted, sent to the appropriate person, and/or assessed to determine whether or not a fee is applicable. The agency's goal was three to five days for processing and fee assessment. Staff performance in this particular area had been erratic due to errors caused by insufficient training and an overly complicated process. After analyzing the work flow, simplifying the procedures, and conducting technical training, productivity increased by approximately 63 percent, which saved the organization about $1 million annually.

Success Story Number 10: U.S. Department of Labor, Wage and Hour Division, San Francisco Region

The Wage and Hour Division of the U.S. Department of Labor was created in 1938 to enforce the Fair Labor Standards Act (FLSA). The FLSA was passed during the Depression, designed to improve working conditions and wages for the nation's workers. The Wage and Hour Division has achieved countless notable successes, including the establishment of a minimum wage and the elimination of child labor. The San Francisco region is one of ten field offices in the Wage and Hour national network and its territory includes California, Nevada, Arizona, and Hawaii. The office operates with a staff of 140 and serves a population of approximately 35 million people. The organization's current responsibilities involve enforcing a number of federal laws dedicated to the protection of the wage earner, including the Consumer Credit Protection Act, the Whistle Blower Statutes, the Migrant and Seasonal Agricultural Workers Protection Act, and the Immigration Reform and Control Act.

Like most federal agencies, the Wage and Hour Division has faced diminishing resources and an ever expanding constituency. After taking a critical look at their organization in the early 1980s, the senior managers at the San Francisco division realized that their operating procedures were unnecessarily complicated. Backlogs and gridlock had become facts of life and the increasing workload offered no hope of any relief. As a result of this agencywide evaluation, TQM became the focus of the organization's systematic efforts to improve quality while providing for a greater degree of employee participation. Not surprisingly, managers in the San Francisco division have come to believe that the concept of employee empowerment is the key to the success of their quality improvement program. As true TQM devotees, members of the organization have invested substantial time and energy into the idea that internal and external customers define quality.

As with other winners of the Federal Quality Institute's Quality Improvement Prototype Award, the San Francisco Wage and Hour Division has documented numerous successful improvement projects, one of which involves its Migrant Housing Inspection Task Force. This group is responsible for visiting migrant labor camps and evaluating the living conditions available for the workers. After discovering several sites (more or less by accident) with particularly squalid living conditions, the investigators took a look at their camp review process. After an examination of the current operating procedures with regard to camp conditions, a district office team formulated a plan for more effective enforcement and education about migrant agricultural labor standards. Key elements of the plan included (1) a bilingual task force that visited labor camp sites; (2) more cooperative work with agencies, such as the State Housing Department and California Legal Assistance; and (3) the use of Labor Camp Registries to target past, present, and potential problem areas. The agency's targeted efforts resulted in thirty-six housing inspections and the assessment of over $66,000 in civil fines. These actions were accomplished in a period of a few days, which is remarkable considering that similar actions in the past would have taken several months.

Another important improvement project involved enforcement issues. In 1991, one district office found itself critically shortstaffed. Personnel were having great difficulty covering their assigned areas and conducting their respective programs, which included community education on child labor laws and enforcement. Part of the problem was that internal regulations required that all investigations be conducted on-site, and as a result, many remote areas were not being covered at all. In response to this problem, a self-managing team was formed that developed the idea of child labor office audits. This system used California state work permits to target potential problem areas, which were then essentially audited by mail, with the employers providing employment records and other requested materials. On-site inspections thus became necessary only to verify sites where actual hazardous conditions were suspected. This new program has greatly improved the agency's ability to effectively monitor large pieces of territory. In one targeted area, two investigators were able to handle fourteen cases, including 101 branch establishments. Their efforts resulted in the discovery of ninety-four child labor violations, for which they were able to assess $106,000 in civil penalties.

Conclusion

As you can see, TQM has been successfully applied in a wide variety of government organizations. Quality improvement projects have resulted in significant cost savings, improved services to agency customers and clients, and measurable improvements in employee morale and productivity. Although the process of bringing TQM into an organization is rarely easy, we believe that these and earlier examples demonstrate that it can be rewarding. Most government organizations are in the first few years of learning and implementing TQM. Organizations that show major improvements and radical changes in the way they do their work have been implementing TQM for five to eight years or more. The final chapter of this book, Chapter Nine, presents some of the keys to success with TQM.

CHAPTER 9

Making TQM Work
in Government:
Real-World Strategies

In his study of bus drivers in San Francisco, S. Leonard Syme observed: "The driver leads his life according to a schedule that, in San Francisco, cannot be met. There's no way you can drive any segment of the bus route on time even on a Sunday morning in a race car. Nevertheless, when the drivers are late, which they usually are, they get demerits from their supervisors. Drivers try to beat the clock by skipping food, rest, and bathroom stops during their twelve-hour workday" (Ornstein and Sobel, 1987, p. 201). Investigators in San Francisco "found exceedingly high rates of hypertension among the bus drivers." They looked at the "high-demand, low-control" nature of the bus driver's work as a probable major contributor to the high blood pressures (Ornstein and Sobel, 1987, p. 200).

Syme goes on to mention changes being considered, such as involving the drivers in developing bus schedules and creating rest stop locations that will enable drivers to talk with their peers, because the driver is socially isolated even while surrounded by passengers all day (Ornstein and Sobel, 1987).

This may appear to be an extreme example, but we have seen these kinds of situations in many government organiza-

198

tions. There is a good chance that you have similar systems in your agency, for example:

- Remember the group whose correspondence went through eleven levels of review, who felt they could not get it right even if their lives depended on it.
- Think about the people in the procurement office who have to process 33 percent of the year's work in the last month of the year.
- Consider the private sector people trying to guess what an agency wants in samples and reports.
- Calculate how many reports people in your organization are preparing where they do not know how the report will be used and they are not allowed to talk with the customer to find out.
- Reflect on how people feel when they have to complete a report or respond to correspondence in one day, because the request took nine days to reach them.

We point this out to emphasize once again that nearly all productivity problems are created by systems of work, created by management. What could the bus drivers do within their system? What could the workers do in the examples above? As a manager you influence the development of the system you work in, so change has to begin with you.

Bringing It All Together

If you are just starting to implement TQM, on your early projects recognize that you cannot remember all the concepts, tools, admonitions, and suggestions at the outset—if ever. Second, competence and understanding come through use, so your proficiency will only improve through practice. Understanding of the theory or core concepts of TQM is also important, because that is what will guide you as you make specific choices. It will also help you to recognize where you have gone off course so that you can make corrections.

Start with the Customer

Based on our own experience and work with many government programs, they rarely consider the customer before they create a labyrinth of constraints. These constraints are built from interpreting the legislation and executive orders, as well as standard personnel, procurement, facility, and budget procedures. Only then, if at all, does government typically consider the customer. As we indicated in Chapter Two, we frequently design an entire process without talking with the customer of that process. Or if we do, we do it at the end to see how the customer likes or understands what we have concocted. Underlying this behavior is a belief that we are the experts and we know what our customers need. When you are working on a problem, or trying to improve a process, you need to ask, "Where is our customer diagnosis?"

Let Your Suppliers Help You

Is your supplier another office or agency? Are your suppliers contractors, consultants, vendors? Do you process applications from the public and operate as if they are not too bright? When people fill out these applications, they are your suppliers. If you are going to do your job, you need them to do a good job of supplying you with information. Do you know how they prepare the material they send to you? How are they supposed to know what you need? Do you have a current flow chart of their part of the process and how it links to your part of the same process? You can only do this by talking with your suppliers. That means more than a general "chit-chat"—it means sitting down with them in improvement sessions around a flow chart or cause-and-effect diagram, including them in the design phase of a program, project, or procedure, not just at the end.

Your suppliers know a lot about their business or function. Let them help you as a professional, instead of you, as an amateur in their business, telling them what to do. For example, we have seen many government people tell the print shop the exact way they wanted something reproduced. An alternative is to discuss with the print shop what you are trying to accomplish so they can tell you which graphics and reproduction services and technologies are most suitable for your purposes. If you get them in at the front end, they will also save you rework by enabling you to prepare the materials for reproduction correctly the first time.

Build Trust and Amnesty and Make It Possible to Tell the Truth

We have given you examples of why the worker knows best the obstacles and barriers that keep him or her from doing the work right the first time. How are you going to elicit worker involvement?

Workers will rarely sit in a room with supervisors or managers and in general conversation contribute what they know, but training in some of the basic quality tools gives them a voice. In a well-run quality improvement project, they will talk about what happens at specific steps in their work process. They know what can go wrong, or sometimes what can make it easier, faster, less expensive to do.

You do have to provide a place to meet and a few supplies, and, most important, time for meetings. We believe training and using the workers' abilities in a quality approach to work and then putting many of their recommendations into place does more than create improvements. Workers are recognized as being able to think, to contribute, and even to improve the design of the program or work, to see their ideas implemented and their contribution recognized by their fellow workers. This is a solid way of treating workers with respect.

An important aspect of genuinely involving the worker is to recognize that you can only improve from where you are. Therefore, you need to be able to determine where you are or how you are performing a particular service or product or process. Typically we have found that people and organizations kid themselves about their performance and do not even try to measure it.

We have two points to emphasize here. First, if your current performance is 120 days to complete a permit, then that is what you will have to improve from, regardless of what the goal is. If you get down to 108 days to complete a permit, that is real progress and a 10 percent improvement. Celebrate it, but do not stop. Do not stop when you get to 90 days either.

Our second point is that you have to make it okay to admit how you are doing now. Many bosses and workers rationalize that they are doing okay. Without an atmosphere of amnesty, neither workers or managers will be willing to reveal areas needing improvement. Improvement teams working on a specific process facilitate this kind of exchange. The fear that Deming says we must drive out is real. Recall the incident earlier where the worker could not allow the real time her boss took to approve her work to be put down on the flow chart. If you remember the adage "It's not who did this, but what went wrong in the process," raising problems encountered in the work becomes more acceptable. Use of the fishbone, flow chart, and control charts reveals problems in a more objective and less personally threatening way.

Build Quality into the Process

Picture a division chief, head of a 250-person organization. He has just been shown a way to clarify how certain correspondence needs to be done, so that the workers can prepare it right the first time, saving rework, frustration, and delays. He strides over to his conference table laden with piles of papers and pulls out one folder. Defiantly he shows us where a word has been omitted in an outgoing letter. "That's why I have to review everything that goes out of this place," he says. Despite an orientation to TQM, he clearly does not understand *that you cannot inspect quality into a process.* Inspections only identify rejects. The critical question to be discussed in situations like this is, How can we create a process that gets it right every time? Or, How can we increase the number of times we get it right, by improving the process?

We recommend that you avoid reviewing, concurring, approving, and checking work. They are all forms of inspection and you should call the person doing those things an inspector. The question to ask inspectors is, "What are you inspecting for? Why not tell workers what you are looking for so they can get it right without your having to inspect?"

Where others inspect your work, keep data on the reasons for the rejections or changes. Then you can work to change the process so it can be done right the first time. The question is, "Why are they getting it wrong?" Do they know what is required? Have they been trained as necessary? We are dismayed by how little training in government is aimed at improving performance.

Policy Makers and Planners Must Focus on the Field

Policy, legislative, budget, and other staff offices are among the worst offenders in ignoring how programs will be operated or implemented. Involving the people who will have to do the work has been a rarity until recently. This is especially true in the design stages where only analysts are allowed to play.

Often when someone from a high-level staff office meets with a staff member from the legislature, it is time to worry. Neither one knows the real work involved in implementing policy. We in government sometimes resemble the auto companies that until recently had the executives create the car concept, the designers design it, the engineers develop the specifications, and then passed it on to the manufacturing specialists who had to find a way to make it. Then marketing and the dealers had to sell it and maintain it. Each process was done in sequence and then "thrown over the transom" to the next department. We see a similar process in government as programs move from policy to legislation to operations. Even during operations the same pattern is repeated when headquarters plans the program and then ships it to the field to be implemented. Except for a perfunctory meeting or two to react to the proposed plan, there is often little or no field input.

Ford Motor Company and other auto companies have been using a team approach in recent years. Everyone from the customer to the mechanic who will have to repair the car someday is in at the conception and design stage. Some results of this approach have been the Taurus and the Sable, and at General Motors, the Saturn.

We urge those of you who manage or are part of a staff office to reach out to include the people who have to do the work. Find out how work gets done: What do frontline workers really face when they process a permit? How do they inspect facilities in the field? What kind of problems do their customers face . . . grantees, states, regulated companies? What ideas do they have for improving the process? Involving frontline workers not only gives you greater credibility when you come up with your recommendation but enlists those who have helped you to develop the plan to work hard to make "their" plan work.

This is not easy to do because most staff of this type have built a well-deserved reputation as theorists who do not know or care about operating people or implementation. The line program personnel will be suspicious and you will have to earn their trust.

Keeping TQM on Track

Most management innovations fall short of the impact advertised by their proponents. PPBS, ZBB, MBO, MIS, and TQM are not magic—achieving management excellence is an ongoing struggle. Adding a new management and budgeting system involves a complex process of organizational learning. People must learn the new routines and must be convinced of the logic and benefit of new practices. TQM is a far more profound change than simply adding a new reporting or budgeting system: it is a new way of thinking about work; people do not change the way they think about work overnight.

Expecting a Long Process

Most of what we have learned about work is learned over a long period of time by watching and imitating the work practices of others. Most of us are not very self-conscious about the way we work. Tasks, frequently created by a phone call, memo, or meeting, are given to us by the person we work for or are self-initiated in order to satisfy some perceived need. Once we are given a task, we think a little about how we might approach the work and then begin to do it. We look to see if we have done anything like this before and imitate the way we performed the similar task. TQM seeks to take this nearly unconscious set of practices and bring them to the forefront of our consciousness.

What was automatic now becomes subject to detailed analysis and, it is hoped, improvement. Learning to stop and think about how we work is not easy, and most organizations will require some time to build this kind of analysis into their culture and standard operating procedures.

As we indicated in Chapter Four, culture and SOPs are important because TQM does not simply mean that individuals learn to think about their own work; TQM also teaches groups of people who are involved in collective tasks to think about the way their tasks interact and how they work as a group. The time and resources needed to analyze work have to be made available as part of the normal process of doing the work. This is not to say that we plan and anticipate everything we do and refuse to participate in emergency quick-turnaround tasks. It means that everything is not an emergency, and even quick-turn-around tasks can be subjected to analysis to improve response.

TQM requires a great deal of change in an organization's practices, and we should not expect that this change will take place quickly. You will achieve some quick successes, encounter resistance, and find the adoption of TQM as a way of work an uneven process of two steps forward and one step back.

Balancing Persistence and Pragmatism

While you are attempting to get your staff to adopt this new way of working, your organization will still need to complete its assigned tasks. Expect a long transition period, lasting several years, where you gradually replace one way of working with another. During this period, it is important to look for opportunities to reinforce TQM in everyday tasks, but also assume that a great deal of your organization's work will proceed in the "old" way.

You will still need to rely on people who refuse to analyze their own work or who do not recognize the need for change. Sometimes you will need to insist on work analysis and customer communication and teach through your suggestions and questions. For example, simply asking whether a manager or group has considered the customer's needs is not good enough; you will need more detail. Ask about the customer's preferences and needs; ask how your people plan to respond to those needs; encourage serious and constant reflection on the needs.

You cannot close your organization down and cease to produce while you attempt to carry out TQM: normal tasks must continue and standard outputs must be produced. But in the course of this work, ask questions about the products you are given that can only be answered if people are working within the guidelines of TQM, questions such as: Who is the customer for this? What is the customer really asking for? Have you spoken to this customer to determine what he or she really wants? How often have you spoken with the customer? How long does it take to accomplish this task? Who does this work? What steps are involved? How often is the output redone? Who provided you with these data? Did you try to influence their format? These are questions that can be answered only if your staff person has a solid understanding of the real work involved in a particular program or activity.

Be pragmatic and keep your organization productive but also be persistent and constantly ask the type of questions listed above, training and reinforcing your managers and staff to constantly ask the same questions. After a while, everyone in your organization will approach work by first asking these types of questions. At first, many small improvements will be suggested and put in place. These are important: somebody thought them up; some people feel good about their ideas being adopted. When ten, twenty, and thirty improvements are made, people begin to change how they approach work. They become less willing to accept old barriers and delays or rework.

Continuous Training

In implementing TQM, you are attempting nothing short of a paradigm shift in how people work and think about the world of work, so TQM needs constant reinforcement before it becomes infused into an organization's culture. In addition, new people must be trained, and as the organization learns new things about how to work and as it adapts TQM to its own work, additional training will be needed.

A key point is that at its core, TQM is the continuous and rapid revision, implementation, and evaluation of an organization's standard operating procedures. With TQM, the organization is placing itself in the position of being constantly open to, and striving toward, new learning.

In a TQM organization, training is the flip side of work analysis. Think of it as a three-step process:

1. Analyze work processes to improve them.
2. Experiment and adopt new ways of performing tasks.
3. Implement new work processes by educating or training staff to do the work in a new way.

Education or training—teaching and learning—is not a separate, "stand-alone" process; it is integral to an effort to implement new work processes and must be a regular, integrated element of an organization's operation. A TQM organization is constantly analyzing and modifying current work processes. When the people in the organization develop improved ways to perform a task or set of tasks, those ideas must be articulated to the relevant members of the organization. One part of that communication is training.

TQM Should Become Invisible

One indicator that TQM has taken root in an organization is that people stop talking about it as a separate thing: it simply becomes the way *this* organization approaches work. In the first phase of teaching TQM, you must emphasize that it is a visible, identifiable set of practices in order to build the habit. At first, people view applying TQM to their work and improvement projects as extra work. "We are already swamped," they claim. "We don't have time for this stuff." Within a few months they should begin to see and understand that using TQM is not in addition to their work but the way they do their regular work.

It becomes invisible because it is part of the basic fabric of the way the organization works. You will recognize that stage when you pose a "bright idea" to your group and they challenge you by asking for your customer and supplier analysis.

Quality is not the responsibility of the "Office of Quality Management" but is the responsibility of every manager in the organization. We recommend that you avoid establishing and maintaining a permanent "quality organization."

We have seen early quality councils and staffs try to accomplish a quality change by using the old command-and-control approach, which creates success measures and "bean counting" on how many people have been trained, how many councils have been set up, and how many projects are under way. We have talked with too many people who tell us, "All our bosses care about is looking good and not about making genuine improvements or changing the way we work." We recommend that you push people to learn by trying and practicing TQM and prodding them to apply it to their own work. After they have done this for a year, then they may be ready to contribute to a coordinating or support group like a central quality council.

In the short run, form a temporary task force of people within your agency and give them the resources to hire trainers to start the process of teaching your people about TQM. However, all these agencywide efforts can do is plant the seed and expose staff to the core concepts of TQM; in the end, each manager must be motivated to learn about TQM and adapt its needs to the organization's work. Obviously, you need to give some people in your organization responsibility for being the change agents for TQM. What is critical is that this group of individuals work on TQM education and inspiration for only a short period of time because, in our view, it is best if the people assigned with the lead in this area are not devoted full time to TQM. Let these staff maintain their regular work as well.

Teach from Experience

We have found that TQM is best taught by people who are using it in regular day-to-day work. If that "regular work" seems similar to the work that other staffers are engaged in, stories about how TQM can help will seem relevant and important. People learn by analogy and while some people can take examples from one type of organization and apply it to another, most people look for their lessons closer to home.

In the EPA and other government agencies, we notice that training provided by consultants that has focused on the private sector is almost always discredited, or at least heavily discounted, by government staff. Some people are able to make the leap from private to public practices, but many cannot.

Implement Gradually

The traditional TQM dogma is that the entire organization must be trained immediately and simultaneously. Perhaps this can work in the private sector, although we very much doubt it, but if TQM implementation is to be a deep and meaningful change in the organization's culture, it must be spread through the organization in gradual phases.

The language and analytical style of the organization will change. Managers will be asked: "Who is the customer for this work and what do they want from us?" "What type of progress have you made in communicating your needs to your suppliers?" "How is this work now performed?" "What is the current level of performance?" In sum, all of the questions that appear in Exhibit 5.1, the Quality Improvement Project Checklist, enter into the normal dialogue of people working in your organization. Managers expect that the people who work for them will start to think about these issues.

This long and gradual change process requires frequent feedback to make sure that the change is more than superficial and is really becoming part of the organization's culture. Assume that old habits will not die easily. One way to see if you are accomplishing deep and lasting change is to try to project the future of TQM in your organization if you were to leave. Would the new way of working survive your departure? If you are not sure, assume that you still have a long way to go.

If it is to be effective, TQM cannot stand alone. We are not opposed to establishing permanent TQM organizations because we dislike bureaucracy; rather, it is because it is critical that TQM permeate the organization at all levels and in each aspect of day-to-day practice. Each project undertaken should involve, as routine steps, items such as customer and supplier analysis and a description and assessment of current performance levels. At regular intervals those involved in the project should be asking: "Can this work be done any better?" "What does the customer say?" "Did we mention that point to our supplier yesterday?" This way of thinking and working should become so pervasive that people think and say, "Oh, that's no big deal; that's the way we always do things around here."

Keep It Simple

TQM is not statistical process control. TQM is an approach to work that says: think about the work you are doing; analyze the process of performing tasks; attempt to improve those processes. Make sure that the work processes you are improving are producing things that your customer wants. As a customer to your own suppliers, work together with them to clearly define your needs and to establish regular feedback on their performance.

Flow charts, fishbone diagrams, run charts, and pareto charts are simply ways of displaying information. Control charts are often used to analyze variation in work processes and identify sources and effects of improvements. However, tasks can be analyzed and improved without statistics. The core activity is to take an honest look at current performance levels and to use that knowledge of the real work to improve performance.

We have omitted mentioning many TQM concepts and tools. This was done intentionally. Our reasoning is based on experience, observation, and belief. First, in adopting TQM you are introducing a number of new ideas that, like all changes, are difficult to accept or incorporate into the organization's work. Therefore, we think it better to start with a simple form of working with the customer and supplier, using a few analytical tools like flow charts and cause-and-effect diagrams. The concept of working with other members of your organization who are central to your work process is also important. Here we have not tried to duplicate the excellent work done by Peter Scholtes and others in *The Team Handbook*, although there may be too much structure for workers engaged in the early stages of TQM in that source as well.

We believe and have seen that there is so much waste in almost all organizations that sophisticated tools are not needed to achieve major improvements during the first few years. Therefore we advocate that you worry less about optimization at this stage and get visible improvement that the worker can see is helping reduce rework, delay, and frustration.

In addition, people being trained in TQM are overwhelmed when exposed to ten or twenty tools, techniques, and concepts in the usual two- or three-day saturation courses. At first, people are unsure of themselves in using the tools and need to practice a few soon after the training until they gain confidence in their use. They also need to see benefits that flow to them and their work from the use of these tools.

Finally, two things will occur to lead people deeper into TQM concepts and additional tools. A few individuals will become fanatics and read, study, and learn all they can, which will lead them to more advanced concepts and to complex forms of statistical process control. Where this occurs, support it as much as you can. More advanced tools and concepts will also come into play when the need arises. A group has done all they can do to get initial improvements or is stymied on a specific problem and at that point is open to help or to expending the extra effort to move beyond the basics.

We have seen too many TQM efforts that assume that everyone wants to adopt and master the field. TQM advocates and trainers behave as if everyone will have the desire, drive, and intensity of an aspiring Olympic athlete, but most people have more modest goals.

TQM Is Not a Religion

The presence of gurus and a concept of management so all-encompassing that it can be viewed as a paradigm shift can make thoughtful people nervous. We have tried in this book to demythologize TQM, to reduce it to some simple, central core concepts, and to emphasize that the application of these ideas will require different techniques in different types of organizations. We have not offered fourteen points or even ten commandments. This is a "how-to-do-it book," but it is not a cook-book.

We have little patience with people who quote one TQM guru or another to indicate that something an organization is doing is "not correct TQM." This is, of course, utter nonsense. TQM is not a religion—it is a set of useful ideas and tools that managers and workers can use to improve the services and products they create and provide. There is no one, true, absolute way to do this.

Remember That Organizations Are People

In *The Effective Public Manager* (1988), Cohen made the point that "the final ingredient in the recipe for failure is forgetting that organizations are made up of people and that people count. Management can be defined as the art of getting people to do things. Effective management is getting people to do the *right* things" (Cohen, 1988, p. 12).

Motivating Organizational Change

TQM only works if the people within the organization want it to work. Management involves motivating people. This is difficult to do under ordinary circumstances; it is an even greater challenge when you are trying to create a fundamental change in an organization's culture: the definition of work.

Organizational change can only occur at the rate that individual learning takes place. People have different, but definitely finite, capacities to accept new knowledge and change their behaviors. When trying to stimulate large-scale change, it is important to constantly check with the organization's members to see if they are comfortable with what is happening. Ideally, they will be excited about the possible changes; but if they feel threatened by the pace of change, it may be necessary to slow down.

In some instances, when we have seen TQM fail, we have noticed that the people in charge have an almost mechanical concept of what TQM is. They focus more on the analytical component than the human relations dimension. We view TQM as an effort to combine some of the elements of effective human resource management with hard-nosed analysis of organizational performance. For TQM to work, these two dimensions must be kept in balance.

TQM requires an honest analysis of what an organization is producing, how production processes operate, and why they operate as they do. However, this analysis is not just done for its own sake—work analysis is the starting point for work improvement. If creative ideas to improve work are to be developed and *implemented,* staff must be fully involved. Implementation will not occur without enthusiastic staff acceptance of the new work processes. One of the best ways to generate such acceptance is staff involvement to the point that they believe they have invented and own these innovations.

Introducing TQM: A Political Process

One of the critical variables affecting success and failure is the way TQM is introduced into the organization. Efforts to simply mandate TQM from the top down nearly always fail.

As we observe organizations trying to adopt TQM, we are struck by the political nature of the process. TQM seems to have the greatest chance of success when those seeking to institute the change recognize that they must build support for these new ideas throughout the organization. The change process resembles a political campaign, requiring organization, advocacy, and multiple channels of communication. Organization members take cues about TQM from the people they respect in the organization, who are frequently the hardest people to convince that a change needs to be made, whether TQM or anything else. These people convert themselves one by one. Some of the strongest practitioners of TQM that we know were reluctant or slow to embrace TQM; it took as long as a year or eighteen months in a few cases.

If people you respect are advocating TQM, you give it greater credence and are willing to seriously consider using it. A key to success with TQM is to recognize that it cannot be imposed by fiat. Management must devote time and effort to educating staff, bringing them along, and timing the pace of change to match the capacity of the organization.

The Need for Courage

Identifying work process problems and customer needs is only one-third of the TQM process. Developing solutions, or ways to exceed the customer's expectations, is another third of the process. The last third is selling and convincing those involved: your co-workers, other units that are suppliers and customers for your work, and the people upstairs—the bosses. If you do not succeed in the last third, selling change and analyzing work and customers is a waste of time.

This last step requires the courage to seriously question the way the organization currently does business. One of the big advantages of flow charts, cause-and-effect diagrams, and customer and supplier analyses is that they enable you to present contrary information in a less threatening and confrontational way. But when the data show that your unit's on-time delivery is 10 percent, you or the team will have to try to get changes made. It means defending and explaining your data. It means facing up to hostility. It involves pushing on people and bosses who feel they cannot do anything about an SOP, that it is too small to bother with or impossible to change.

We witnessed a recent example. In trying to solve a problem, the managers involved decided that the activity in question should be changed. To get other managers in the hierarchy to pay attention to this activity, they recommended that it be included in their performance standards. Satisfied with themselves, they sat back. We asked, "How many of you know what is in your performance standards?" Two of ten participants raised their hands. Then we asked, "How many of you have your day-to-day or week-to-week behavior affected by what is in your performance standards?" No one raised their hand in answer to that question. Then we asked, "Why are you assuming that putting this in people's standards will bring about the change you want?" This may not sound dramatic, but it does take courage to stop the creation of new forms of waste or to eliminate existing ones.

Another example from our experience was a situation involving a change that the legislature wanted to see in the OUST program. The change was made and all members of the legislature were notified through a fact sheet. Then a manager came in and said that the agency correspondence control office had called and reported that 287 legislators had written requesting that change. These items could not be checked as completed until letters were written to each of them. The staff recognized this as waste and basically asked, "Are we going to do this silly thing, because the system calls for it?" We decided not to do it and did not. We were prepared to explain why and defend our decision.

Of course, there are much larger issues where your people, once trained, will identify various forms of waste. Management must be prepared to fight within the organization to implement employee suggestions for eliminating waste. Your people will watch to see if you even make a serious and sustained effort to do the right thing. This will outweigh all the words, training, banners, and slogans.

We are both dismayed at the many senior executives in government agencies who suffer from a double image. On the one hand, they are comparatively well paid, have lots of education and experience, believe they are essential and special to their agency's mission and program, and are very competent, in fact, outstanding, at their jobs. On the other hand, when confronted with processes and systems that create waste, these same senior managers back off as though they are helpless. We do not believe they are helpless, because TQM does give them an effective way to battle these apparently unassailable systems, practices, rules, and processes.

Continuous and Never-Ending Improvement

If you are a manager, one of your main tasks is to make your organization capable of continuously improving quality, the final aim of TQM. Fortunately you do not have to, and in fact cannot, do this alone. It is hard to explain the power, enthusiasm, and joy in work that flow from having most of the people in the organization working continuously on improvements.

Achieving continuous quality is a long-term commitment that can begin today with small steps. It starts when you determine who your customers are and what they need. It becomes really serious when the people in your organization take a hard look at how the work gets done. It gets exciting when your people start to identify and eliminate waste from the work. You know it is happening when your customers brag about how good your program or service has become. TQM is a way to reinvigorate government, for those who work in it and for those who are served by it.

REFERENCES

Beer, M. *Organization Change and Development: A Systems View.* Santa Monica, Calif.: Goodyear, 1980.

Behn, R. D. "Management by Groping Along." *Journal of Policy Analysis and Management,* 1988, 7(3), 643–663.

Behn, R. D. "Leadership Counts." *Journal of Policy Analysis and Management,* 1989, 8(3), 494–500.

Caiden, G. E. "Ethics in the Public Service." *Public Personnel Management,* 1981, 10, 146–152.

Caves, R. E., and Roberts, M. J. (eds.). *Regulating the Product: Quality and Variety.* Cambridge, Mass.: Ballinger, 1975.

Cohen, S. *The Effective Public Manager: Achieving Success in Government.* San Francisco: Jossey-Bass, 1988.

Cohen, S. "Involving Frontline Employees in State and Local Government Decision-Making." A briefing paper presented to the National Commission on the State and Local Public Service, Albany, New York, July 1992.

Cohen, S., and Brand, R. "The Use of Continuous Quality Improvement Techniques in Government: The Case of the Federal Underground Tank Program." *Public Productivity and Management Review,* 1990, 14(1), 99–114.

Cohen, S., and Kamieniecki, S. *Environmental Regulation Through Strategic Planning.* Boulder, Colo.: Westview Press, 1991.

Contino, R. A., and Giuliano, J. "Productivity Gains Through Employee Participation at the New York City Department of Sanitation." *Public Productivity and Management Review,* 1991, 15(2), 185–190.

Conway, W. E. *The Quality Secret: The Right Way to Manage.* Nashua, N.H.: Conway Quality, 1992.

217

Crosby, P. B. *Quality Is Free: The Art of Making Quality Certain.* New York: McGraw-Hill, 1979.

Crosby, P. B. *Quality Without Tears: The Art of Hassle-Free Management.* New York: McGraw-Hill, 1984.

Deming, W. E. *Some Theories of Sampling.* New York: Dover, 1966.

Deming, W. E. *Quality, Productivity, and Competitive Position.* Cambridge, Mass.: Cambridge University Press, 1982.

Deming, W. E. *Out of the Crisis.* Cambridge, Mass.: Cambridge University Press, 1986.

Dobyns, L., and Crawford-Mason, C. *Quality or Else: The Revolution in World Business.* Boston: Houghton Mifflin, 1991.

Ernst & Young Quality Improvement Consulting Group. *Total Quality: An Executive's Guide for the 1990s.* Homewood, Ill.: Dow Jones–Irwin, 1990.

Evans, J. R. *The Management and Control of Quality.* St. Paul, Minn.: West Publishing, 1989.

Federal Quality Institute. "Quality Improvement Prototype Award—1991. Sacramento Air Logistics Center, Air Force Logistics Command, Department of the Air Force." Washington, D.C.: U.S. Government Printing Office, 1991.

Federal Quality Institute. "Quality Improvement Prototype Award—1992. Defense Contract Management District Northeast, Boston, MA." Washington, D.C.: U.S. Government Printing Office, 1992a.

Federal Quality Institute. "Quality Improvement Prototype Award—1992. Department of Veterans Affairs, Philadelphia, PA." Washington, D.C.: U.S. Government Printing Office, 1992b.

Federal Quality Institute. "Quality Improvement Prototype Award—1992. Public Services and Administration Patent and Trademark Office, Department of Commerce, Arlington, VA." Washington, D.C.: U.S. Government Printing Office, 1992c.

Federal Quality Institute. "Quality Improvement Prototype Award—1992. U.S. Department of Labor, Wage and Hour Division, San Francisco Region." Washington, D.C.: U.S. Government Printing Office, 1992d.

Feigenbaum, A. V. *Total Quality Control.* New York: McGraw-Hill, 1983.

Garvin, D. A. *Managing Quality: The Strategic and Competitive Edge.* New York: Free Press, 1988.

Goldratt, E. M. *Theory of Constraints.* Croton-on-Hudson, N.Y.: North River Press, 1990.

Goldratt, E. M., and Cox, J. *The Goal.* Croton-on-Hudson, N.Y.: North River Press, 1992.

Harrington, H. J. *The Improvement Process: How America's Leading Companies Improve Quality.* New York: McGraw-Hill, 1987.

Hudiburg, J. *Winning with Quality: The Florida Power and Light Story.* White Plains, N.Y.: Quality Resources, 1991.

Hummel, R. P. *The Bureaucratic Experience.* New York: St. Martin's Press, 1977.

Imai, M. *Kaizen: The Key to Japanese Competitive Success.* New York: Random House, 1986.

Ishikawa, K. *Guide to Quality Control.* New York: UNIPUB, 1985.

Juran, J. M. *Juran on Planning for Quality.* New York: Free Press, 1988.

Juran, J. M. *Juran on Quality by Design: The New Steps for Planning Quality into Goods and Services.* New York: Free Press, 1992.

Kaboolian, L., and Barzaley, M. "TQM in the Federal Sector: Discourse, Practices, and Movements." Presented at the annual conference of the Association of Public Policy and Management, San Francisco, 1990.

Koons, P. F. "Getting Comfortable with TQM." *Bureaucrat,* Summer 1991, pp. 35–38.

Kotter, J. P. "What Leaders Really Do." *Harvard Business Review,* May-June 1990, pp. 103–111.

Lawrence, P. R., and Lorsch, J. W. "New Management Job: The Integrator." *Harvard Business Review,* 1967a, *45*(6), 142–151.

Lawrence, P. R., and Lorsch, J. W. *Organization and Environment.* Boston, Mass.: Division of Research, Graduate School of Business Administration, Harvard University, 1967b.

Lynn, L. E., Jr. *Managing the Public's Business.* New York: Basic Books, 1981.

Lynn, L. E., Jr. *Managing Public Policy.* Boston: Little, Brown, 1987.

Maass, R. A. *Supplier Certification: A Continuous Improvement Strategy.* Milwaukee, Wis.: Customer Supplier Technical Committee, 1990.

Mann, N. R. *The Keys to Excellence: The Story of the Deming Philoso-phy.* Los Angeles: Prestwick Books, 1985.

March, J. G., and Simon, H. A. *Organizations.* New York: Wiley, 1958.

Matherly, L. L., and Lasater, H. A. "Implementing TQM in a Hospital." *Quality Progress,* April 1992, pp. 81–84.

Meindel, J. R. "Managing to Be Fair: An Exploration of Values, Motives, and Leadership." *Administrative Science Quarterly,* 1989, *34,* 252–276.

Merton, R. K. "Bureaucratic Structure and Personality." *Social Forces,* 1940, *18,* 560–568.

Mintzberg, H. *The Nature of Managerial Work.* New York: HarperCollins, 1973a.

Mintzberg, H. "Strategy Making in Three Modes." *California Management and Review,* 1973b, *16,* 44–58.

Mintzberg, H. "The Manager's Job: Folklore and Fact." *Harvard Business Review,* Mar.-Apr. 1990, pp.163–176.

Neave, H. R. *The Deming Dimension.* Knoxville, Tenn.: SPC Press, 1990.

Ornstein, R., and Sobel, D. *The Healing Brain.* New York: Simon & Schuster, 1987.

Osborne, D., and Gaebler, T. *Reinventing Government: How the Entrepreneurial Spirit Is Transforming the Public Sector.* Reading, Mass.: Addison-Wesley, 1992.

Patti, R. J. "Organizational Resistance and Change: The View from Below." *Social Service Review,* 1974, *48,* 367–382.

Peace, W. H. "I Thought I Knew What Good Management Was." *Harvard Business Review,* Mar.-Apr. 1986, pp. 59–65.

Peters, T. J. *Thriving on Chaos: Handbook for a Management Revo-lution.* New York: Knopf, 1987.

Rainey, H. G. *Understanding and Managing Public Organizations.* San Francisco: Jossey-Bass, 1991.

Rosenthal, S. R. "Producing Results in Government: Moving Beyond Project Management and Its Limited View of Suc-cess." *Journal of Policy Analysis and Management,* 1989, *8*(1), 110–116.

Sayles, L. R. *Managerial Behavior.* Huntington, N.Y.: Krieger, 1980.

Scherkenbach, W. H. *The Deming Route to Quality and Productivity.* Washington, D.C.: CEEPress Books, 1990.

Scholtes, P. R., and others. *The Team Handbook: How to Use Teams to Improve Quality.* (S. Reynard, ed.) Madison, Wis.: Joiner Associates, 1988.

Schonberger, R. J. *Japanese Manufacturing Techniques: Nine Hidden Lessons in Simplicity.* New York: Free Press, 1982.

Schonberger, R. J. *Building a Chain of Customers.* New York: Free Press, 1990.

Scott, W. B. "Aerospace/Defense Firms See Preliminary Results from Application of TQM Concepts." *Aviation Week and Space Technology,* Jan. 8, 1990, pp. 61–63.

Selznick, P. *TVA and the Grass Roots.* Berkeley: University of California Press, 1949.

Sensenbrenner, J. "Quality Comes to City Hall." *Harvard Business Review,* Mar.-Apr. 1991, pp. 64–75.

Shingo, S. *Study of TOYOTA Production System from Industrial Engineering Viewpoint.* Tokyo: Japan Management Association, 1981.

Shingo, S. *Non-Stock Production: The Shingo System for Continuous Improvement.* Cambridge, Mass.: Productivity Press, 1988.

Smith, M. R. *Qualitysense: Organizational Approaches to Improving Product Quality and Service.* New York: AMACOM, 1979.

Stalk, G., Jr., and Hout, T. M. *Competing Against Time.* New York: Free Press, 1990.

Thomas, A. B. "Does Leadership Make a Difference to Organizational Performance?" *Administrative Science Quarterly,* 1988, *33,* 388–400.

Townsend, P. L. *Commit to Quality.* New York: Wiley, 1986.

Walton, M. *The Deming Management Method.* New York: Dodd, Mead, 1986.

Weber, M. "Characteristics of a Bureaucracy." In M. Weber, *From Max Weber: Essays in Sociology* (H. H. Gerth and C. W. Mills, trans.). New York: Oxford University Press, 1946.

Wheeler, D. J., and Chambers, D. S. *Understanding Statistical Process Control.* (2nd ed.) Knoxville, Tenn.: SPC Press, 1992.

Wilson, J. Q. *Bureaucracy: What Government Agencies Do and Why They Do It.* New York: Basic Books, 1989.

INDEX